WOMEN *for* WOMEN
International

share

A book of joy – Women for Women International began with a commitment on the part of a single individual to contribute in some way to the global community. The underlying message of this cookbook, which celebrates the work of the charity, is exactly that simple: For all our apparent diversity—as individuals, societies, and nations—our actions, however small, have an exponential influence in the world through our shared humanity.

Nothing more beautifully conveys our interdependence than the food we eat. Access to wholesome food is critical to whether we merely survive… or thrive. Food builds our physical resilience, brings us joy, and strengthens our bonds with friends and family. It maintains our connection to the seasons, and generates employment, wealth, and economic stability. What we choose to eat and how we choose to prepare it reflect our ancestral traditions and cultural heritage, as well as our abundant creativity. Food unites us globally.

The individuals whose recipes are featured in this cookbook are all actively engaged in a range of humanitarian causes. Their contribution and yours, through purchasing this book, directly support Women for Women International in its work with women in war-torn countries around the world. It is their focus on women's inner strength and resourcefulness, that has drawn me to their work. As a mother and wife, I believe in the critical role women play in our family's stability and future.

This book includes dishes from world-class chefs and influential humanitarians, as well as lesser-known heroes and the women whose lives have been improved by the charity. The recipes draw on the freshest of ingredients to produce simple yet delicious food, and the chapters reflect the importance of caring for our personal well-being, nurturing our loved ones, supporting our community by developing fair and sustainable trade and, last but not least, uniting in celebration.

Take time to enjoy the food and read the stories. Welcome friends and family to your table. Join me—in celebration of our shared humanity.

Bon Appetit!

WOMEN *for* WOMEN
International

You can change the world, one woman at a time

Women for Women International (WfWI) works with women in **Afghanistan, Bosnia and Herzegovina, the Democratic Republic of Congo, Iraq, Kosovo, Nigeria, Rwanda and South Sudan,** where war and conflict have devastated both lives and communities. The programs run by the charity enable these women to move from victims, to survivors, to active citizens.

In a world where 70 per cent of those living on less than $1 per day are female, investing in women is crucial to achieving broader, long-term development goals – from eradicating extreme poverty and hunger, to improving access to education and reducing child mortality. As the hallmark of a civilized society, the well-being of women has critical implications for communities and, ultimately, nations as a whole. This is particularly true in war and post-war countries. Women are disproportionately affected by conflict; they are targeted for rape and violence, they are forced from their homes, they lose husbands and children and often become the sole providers for their families. Yet despite the atrocities and brutalities women endure, **their overriding courage, strength, and hope continue to sustain them and inspire us all.**

Since its founding by Zainab Salbi in 1993, WfWI has helped over 400,000 women. When women enroll in its one-year program, they receive business and vocational skills training, rights awareness, health education, and financial and emotional support, as well as assistance accessing capital and markets.

Women participants meet others in similar situations to their own, often providing the first opportunity for them to share their fears, hopes, and dreams for a different future. The social network and community that develop can give them a sense of support, strength, and power.

All of this is made possible with the support of sponsors – women and men across the world who form a one-to-one connection with WfWI's program participants. In addition to providing a monthly financial contribution to help cover the costs of training, sponsors can provide essential emotional support for these women, as they know someone else believes in them and their future.

As the women move forward, they are not the only ones to benefit from the support of WfWI. Sponsors frequently say how much their own lives have been enriched by connecting with a "sister." This connection is at the heart of WfWI. The organization has helped women survivors move towards economic self-sufficiency by providing access to economic and social opportunities that bring independence and respect. For each woman helped, up to five others benefit – an estimated 2.16 million family members since WfWI was founded.

It is WfWI's belief that lasting change can only be achieved when women have access to both knowledge and resources. In providing women survivors of war with the tools necessary to move from crisis and poverty to stability and self-sufficiency, we create viable and long-lasting change in communities.

a fair share...

Women for Women International was awarded the 2006 Conrad Hilton Humanitarian Award, becoming the first women's organization to receive this honour.

WOMEN *for* WOMEN
International
well-being
healthy, everyday recipes

Contents

WOMEN for WOMEN
International

share

The cookbook that celebrates
our common humanity

Foreword by Meryl Streep
Edited by Alison Oakervee
Food photography by Philip Webb

Kyle Books

To the Women for Women International participants, staff and sponsors, in honor of their day-to-day courage, determination and generosity.

Published in 2013 by Kyle Books
an imprint of Kyle Cathie Limited
www.kylebooks.com
Distributed by National Book Network
4501 Forbes Blvd., Suite 200
Lanham, MD 20706
Phone: (800) 462-6420
Fax: (301) 429-5746
custserv@nbnbooks.com
First published in Great Britain in 2013
by Kyle Books

general.enquiries@kylebooks.com
www.kylebooks.com

10 9 8 7

ISBN 978-1-906868-87-1

Concept and Development Team:
Lauri Pastrone, Tracy Craighead,
Bette Anne Berg, Alison Oakervee,
Ruth Tyson

Women for Women International UK:
Brita Fernandez Schmidt

Food Editor: Alison Oakervee
Design & Art Direction: Ruth Tyson
Food Photographer: Philip Webb
Prop Stylist: Iris Bromet
Food Stylists: Joss Herd, Danny Maguire
and Bianca Nice
Production: Nic Jones and Gemma John
Editor: Judith Hannam
Editorial Assistant: Tara O'Sullivan

Recipe on page 159 taken from
The Cook's Companion by Stephanie Alexander,
2nd Edition, published by Lantern (Penguin Group
(Australia)), 2004

Recipe on page 183 taken from *Jamie's America*
by Jamie Oliver, published by Penguin (Michael
Joseph), 2009

Lyrics on page 195 from "14 Black Paintings" ©
2012 Peter Gabriel – Courtesy of petergabriel.com
Recipe on page 195 – © Peter Gabriel. Courtesy
of petergabriel.com

Recipe on page 206 taken from *Plenty* by Yotam
Ottolenghi, published by Random House (Ebury),
2010

Recipe on page 209 taken from
*Hunger for Freedom: The Story of Food in the Life
of Nelson Mandela* by Anna Trapido, published
by Jacana Media in association with the Nelson
Mandela Foundation, Johannesburg, 2008

Recipes on page 218 taken from *River Cottage
Every Day* by Hugh Fearnley-Whittingstall,
published by Bloomsbury (2009),
www.bloomsbury.com

Library of Congress Control Number: 2013930410

Colour reproduction by ALTA London
Printed and bound in China by Toppan Leefung
Printing Ltd

*All photographs by Philip Webb except
for the following:
Lynne Abercrombie/Getty Images, page 84
Ceerwan Aziz, page 194
Irene Becker/Getty Images, page 154
Bette Anne Berg, page 248
Tracy Craighead, pages 48–49, 58, 172, 174,
186–187, 213, 236–237, 248
Robin Cross/Article 25 page 112
Nick Haddow, page 6
Millie Harvey, page 250
David Loftus, page 182
David James, pages 56–57, 96, 136
Lauri Pastrone, pages 90, 248
Heathcliff O'Malley, pages 8–9
Lekha Singh, pages 16, 18, 104–105
Brian Sokol, pages 28–29, 40
Les Stone, end papers and pages 100, 124,
140–141, 198
Danin Tulic/Getty Images, page 64
Jenn Warren, pages 10–11, 38
Simon Wheeler, pages 24, 52, 63, 72–73,76,
94–95, 110, 122–123, 130, 131, 138, 168, 176,
177, 247
Images on pages 2, 30, 70, 83, 128, 132, 152 and
164–165 kindly supplied by Women for Women
International Field Staff

"Africa is bursting with hopeful, good news stories. They just don't get covered as much as the bad news. So I derive my inspiration from the knowledge that wars can be ended and, once given a chance, Africans can build their own peace and future in startlingly effective ways. I know — I am a witness."

John Prendergast

Protein breakfast smoothie

2 bananas, chopped
²/₃ cup fresh blueberries
²/₃ cup fresh strawberries
5–10 baby carrots (optional)
1 scoop of vegetable
protein powder (optional)
2 tablespoons almond
or peanut butter
1 tablespoon flaxseed oil
water or fruit juice, to taste

I recently learned that I had too little protein in my diet, especially in the mornings. So I consulted an expert on these matters, the wonderful Dr. Mark Hyman, who did wonders for my former boss, President Clinton. This smoothie has vitamins, protein, and none of the allergens (dairy, gluten) that cause me and so many others all kinds of pain and inflammation. It has a little more sugar than my buddy Dr. Hyman would recommend, but after I gave up nondairy ice cream, I had to hang onto something with a little extra sweetness in it. Mission accomplished on all fronts!

Prepare 5 minutes | **Serves** 2

1 Place the chopped banana and berries in a blender with the carrots (if using). Blend until smooth. Add the protein powder (if using) with the nut butter and flaxseed oil and give a final blend to combine. Add a little water or juice to adjust the consistency to your choice.
2 Pour into a glass and serve.

Lemon and mint infusion

2 slices lemon
2 sprigs fresh mint

Prepare 2 minutes | **Serves** 1

1 For a refreshing start to the day place the lemon and mint into a heatproof glass and cover with boiling water. Allow to steep for 2 minutes before drinking.

Apple, carrot and beet juice

2 apples
3 carrots, scrubbed
1 beet, peeled
¼ lemon, skin removed
(or to taste)
½ inch piece fresh ginger
(optional)

Prepare 5 minutes | **Serves** 1

1 Place a glass in the freezer to chill. Cut the fruit, vegetables and ginger (if using) into small chunks and push through the feeder of a juicer. Pour the juice into the chilled glass and drink immediately.

Annie Lennox: Porridge

²/₃ cup steel-cut oats
or rolled oats
salt
3 cups milk or water,
or equal parts milk and water
milk or cream, to serve

Toppings (optional)
toasted coconut
brown sugar
honey
maple syrup
ground cinnamon
grated lemon zest
raisins

This recipe, a Scots staple, is very simple and the perfect way to get a head start on a freezing, windblown, rain-swept day. The purist's porridge always has salt—with maybe the addition of a little bit of cream—but it can be a great base for all kinds of delicious toppings, such as toasted coconut, brown sugar, honey, maple syrup, cinnamon, lemon rind, raisins... It's cheap, it's nutritious, it's comforting, and it makes you glow!

Prepare 5 minutes | **Cook** 15 minutes | **Serves** 2

1 Place the oats in a large heavy-bottomed pan with a generous pinch of salt. Pour in the milk or water and bring to a boil over medium heat, stirring continually with a traditional spurtle or wooden spoon.

2 When the porridge starts to thicken, reduce the heat and simmer until the oats are cooked through and the porridge is smooth, stirring occasionally with the spurtle or wooden spoon to stop it sticking to the pan. Serve with a little cold milk or cream poured over the top and with a topping of your choice, or a spoonful of the spiced fruit compote (see below).

Spiced fruit compote

3 fruit tea bags
1–2 teaspoons honey
½ cinnamon stick
a pinch of ground allspice
2 cups dried mixed fruit
(such as apricots, apples, pears,
prunes, figs, and cranberries),
roughly chopped
plain yogurt, to serve

Prepare 5 minutes | **Cook** 12-15 minutes, plus infusing | **Serves** 2

1 Place the tea bags in a pan, pour in 1 ¼ cup boiling water, and stir in the honey. Add the cinnamon stick and allspice. Bring to a boil and simmer for 5 minutes. Add the mixed fruit and then simmer for another 5 minutes. Remove from the heat and leave to steep until ready to serve. Remove the tea bags and cinnamon stick before serving.

2 Serve spooned over porridge or on its own with plain yogurt.

"Whatever you do, do it out of passion.
Don't think about rewards, think about what you're doing for its own value."
Annie Lennox

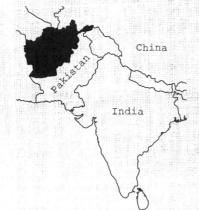

China

Pakistan

India

AFGHANISTAN

Average WfWI participant

Age: 18-24

Married: 59% / Widowed: 7% / Single: 34%

Children: 4 / No. in household: 10

Literate: 14% / No formal education: 86%

Huma's Story

Under the Taliban, working in a beauty parlor was unacceptable. But since 2003 hundreds of women have broken cultural barriers to participate in Beauty Parlor Training in Women for Women International programs in Kabul, Parwan, and Kapisa provinces. Equipped with these new vocational skills, the participants have been able to find steady jobs that generate income to improve the lives of their families and the stability of their communities.

"I used to dream of one day working in my own beauty parlor when I grew up, but when I was 12 I was told by my father that I had to marry a man 28 years my senior. My childhood was over. My husband and I had three daughters. Then, in 2008, he caught an infection and couldn't get the right medical care. He died. I was just 20.

My husband had been the one to provide for us. Like many Afghani girls, I had never been allowed to go to school and had no training. But a year after my husband's death, I learned from a village elder that the Kabul chapter of Women for Women International was taking more women into their program. I hoped that by learning some skills I could find work. I never imagined that beauty training would be offered and was thrilled when I was accepted.

In the evenings, when my housework is complete, I share what I have learned with my daughters-including what I have been taught about the rights of women, rights that are now part of our national constitution. One day I will own my own beauty parlor, but for now I am happy working in one in Kabul and taking care of my daughters. I now know that women can gain skills and learn about rights that have been ignored by our society. This makes me hopeful for the future.

All of the women in my group of 20 are determined that education will give our daughters a better future. Even though it is still dangerous for girls to go to school, we know that education will change things for them. Their lives will be different."

AFGHANISTAN

Population: 30,419,928

Square km: 652,230

GDP per capita: $1000

Unemployment: 35%

Life expectancy:
Female: 51 years / Male: 48 years

Conflict dates: 2001-present/ongoing

Total no. killed: 29,150+

Estimated military deaths: 14,450+

Estimated civilian deaths: 14,700+

Internally displaced persons: 447,550

Recipe from Afghanistan

The varied climate of Afghanistan allows for an abundance of crops throughout the seasons. Historically, it was one of the world's greatest food traders and, when not at war, the country has the potential to be totally self-sufficient. Kandahar is celebrated for its fabled pomegranates, but other fruits-grapes, apricots, berries, and plums-are also plentiful, as are nuts and seeds such as walnuts, pistachios, almonds, peanuts, and pine nuts. In the temperate climate of Nangarhar province, orange and olive groves flourish. Afghani food is known for its contrasting tastes, and for being neither spicy nor bland. Herbs and spices include mint, saffron, coriander, cardamom, and black pepper, which are used to flavor the preferred meats of lamb and chicken.

Bichak

These triangular stuffed pastries are served either on their own as appetizers, or with tea. They can also be made with paneer, a type of cheese, or as a sweet option with fruit purée.

Prepare 1 hour, plus 1 hour rising
| **Cook** 50 minutes | **Makes** 24

For the dough
3 cups bread flour, plus extra for dusting
1 teaspoon salt
1 teaspoon or 1 package active dry yeast
1 egg, beaten, plus 2 egg yolks
1 tablespoon oil

For the filling
2-3 tablespoons vegetable oil
2 onions, finely chopped
1 lb ground lamb or beef
salt and freshly ground black pepper

1 Combine the flour with the salt in a large mixing bowl, stir in the yeast, then make a well in the center of the mixture and pour in ⅔ cup lukewarm water. Beat the whole egg and add it to the mixture along with the oil. Stir with a wooden spoon to mix the ingredients and bring the dough together.

2 Put the dough on a floured work surface and knead for about 10 minutes, adding extra flour as needed, until the dough is no longer sticking to your hands and is silky and elastic. Place the dough in a large, lightly oiled bowl. Cover with plastic wrap and leave in a warm place for 45 minutes-1 hour or until doubled in size.

3 While the dough is rising, make the meat filling. In a large frying pan, heat the oil over medium-high heat. Add the onions and cook for about 5 minutes or until they are softened and translucent. Stir in the ground lamb or beef and cook until the meat is well browned and cooked through, 5-10 minutes. Drain off any excess fat, and season to taste with salt and freshly ground black pepper. Remove from the heat and allow to cool completely

4 Preheat the oven to 350° F. Punch the dough down with your fist and put onto a lightly floured work surface. Cut the dough in two and roll half into a rectangle about ¼ inch thick. Then, using a round pastry cutter 3-4 inches in diameter, cut out 12 disks. Place 1 or 2 tablespoons of the meat mixture into the center of each disk. Fold the top right and left sides of the disk to the center, and bring the lower side up to the center, pinching the edges together to form a triangular seam. Repeat with the remaining dough and filling.

5 Place the bichak on a greased baking sheet. Beat the egg yolks with a little water and brush the top of each pastry with the egg wash. Bake for 35-40 minutes, or until the pastries are golden brown and cooked through.

Paul McCartney: Super vegetable salad

8oz baby new potatoes, halved

1 cup (4oz) green beans, trimmed
and halved

2 carrots, peeled and
cut into sticks

1½ cups broccoli, cut into
small florets

1 Romaine lettuce heart, chopped

3 scallions, sliced

28 cherry or grape tomatoes,
halved

salt and freshly ground
black pepper

For the dressing

2 tablespoons olive oil

1 tablespoon red wine vinegar

1 teaspoon Dijon mustard

1 teaspoon maple syrup,
to taste (optional)

This is a fantastic warm salad that can accompany whatever you're in the mood for—here I've suggested tofu, but you could just as easily serve it with a veggie burger or vegetarian sausage. You can also vary the steamed vegetables according to what's in season.

Prepare 10 minutes | **Cook** 15 minutes | **Serves** 4

1 Place the potatoes in a pan of cold water, place the steamer above them, cover and bring to a boil, then simmer for 15 minutes. After 5 minutes, add the beans and carrots to the steamer. After 10 minutes, add the broccoli.

2 Meanwhile, place the lettuce in a bowl with the scallions and tomatoes. In a separate bowl whisk together the ingredients for the dressing, and set aside.

3 When the potatoes are ready, drain them and add them to the lettuce along with the steamed vegetables. Season, toss with the dressing and serve.

Cook's tip

To make a more substantial salad, serve with tofu. Combine ²/₃ cup cornmeal with a handful of chopped herbs of your choice on a plate. Heat a little olive oil in a frying pan. Cube or slice 8oz tofu, dip into the herb and polenta mix, and then cook until golden. Scatter over the top of the vegetable salad and serve.

"Each woman has a pearl inside of her that cannot be hidden.
They must work to let it appear and surprise everybody."

Rihab, WfWI Iraq participant

"Slavery is a far greater problem than it has ever been. I believe it is down to everyone to play their part in forcing through the change we want to see."

Julia Immonen

Pan-fried fish with a dill, mint and fava bean pilaf

2 tablespoons olive oil

1 onion, peeled and finely chopped

1½ cups long grain rice, rinsed

2½ cups chicken or fish stock

2 tablespoons extra virgin olive oil, plus extra to serve

4 sustainable fish steaks, such as line-caught tuna, each about 7oz and 3 inches thick

14oz can artichoke hearts, drained and sliced

²/₃ cup fava beans, cooked and shelled

½ cup dill, finely chopped

½ cup mint, finely chopped

2 scallions, finely chopped

½ preserved lemon, finely chopped

1 lemon, cut into wedges

salt and freshly ground black pepper

In December 2011 I was part of a team of five women who rowed 3,000 miles across the Atlantic Ocean to raise awareness of human trafficking. Our campaign was called Row for Freedom. When we arrived at Port St Charles after our 45-day journey, all of us craved fresh, simple food. This delicious dish of tuna steaks with fresh herbs, is exactly what we wanted.

Prepare 15 minutes | **Cook** 35 minutes | **Serves** 4

1 Heat the olive oil in a pan over low heat, add the onion, and cook until soft but not colored. Add the rice and stir to coat with the oil, then cook for another 5 minutes, making sure the onion does not color.

2 Add the stock, increase the heat, and bring to a boil, then simmer for 5–7 minutes until the stock is almost absorbed. Reduce the heat to low, cover the pan, and cook for 15 minutes until all the stock has been absorbed. Don't stir.

3 Meanwhile, heat the extra virgin olive oil in a large frying pan. When it is hot add the fish steaks and cook for 2 minutes on each side, or to your liking. Season with salt and freshly ground black pepper.

4 When the rice is cooked, gently stir in the artichoke hearts, fava beans, dill, mint, scallions, and preserved lemon. Serve the tuna steak with the rice, squeeze in some lemon juice, and drizzle with extra virgin olive oil.

"I grew up in the Judeo-Christian tradition where we painted our prophets on ceilings and sealed our saints in stained glass. But here on earth, we have living, breathing human beings in our midst whose determination and valor in the face of overwhelming danger challenge us to take up the torch for a more decent society."

Kerry Kennedy

Kerry Kennedy: Hearty chicken soup

2 tablespoons butter

2 tablespoons olive oil

3 medium onions, peeled and quartered

4 carrots, peeled and cut into chunks

4 parsnips, peeled and cut into chunks

2 ribs celery, halved

4 leeks, washed and sliced

8 peppercorns

1 bay leaf

4 sprigs fresh thyme

2 sprigs rosemary

4 sprigs tarragon

3 lb whole chicken, cut into 8 pieces (or a mix of thighs and drumsticks)

1–1.5 quarts chicken stock

½ cup fresh cilantro

salt and freshly ground black pepper

I've always loved that chicken soup is a meal you can find on dinner tables around the world—whether it's Tom Kha Gai, Sopa de Pollo, or Matzoh Ball. I come back to this recipe again and again because of all the happy memories I have of sitting down to enjoy it with family and friends, and especially my three daughters.

Prepare 15 minutes | **Cook** 2¼ hours | **Serves** 4

1 Heat the butter and olive oil together in a large pan over low heat. Add the onions and cook for 5 minutes, stirring, until softened. Add the remaining vegetables, the herbs (except the cilantro), and the peppercorns and cook for another 5 minutes, stirring occasionally.

2 Add the chicken pieces and enough of the chicken stock to cover all of the ingredients. Cover and bring to a boil, then reduce the heat and simmer, uncovered, stirring occasionally, for 2 hours. Skim off any foam that develops, remove and discard the herb stems, season to taste, and serve, topped with the fresh cilantro leaves.

Cook's tip

To make it easy to remove the herbs and peppercorns at the end of cooking, tie the herbs together with a piece of kitchen twine to form a bouquet garni and place the peppercorns in the center of a square of cheesecloth and tie the edges together to form a pouch. To make this soup more substantial, serve it with cooked rice, mashed potatoes or crusty bread to help soak up all the flavors.

"When trying to deal with complex and daunting situations such as the environment, the pathway to success can often seem a long way away. My inspiration comes from those who don't waver under these conditions and continue to be curious, dream big, and stimulate real world solutions."

David Mayer de Rothschild

Sprouts with avocado and lime

3 tablespoons olive oil

14oz firm tofu, cut into ¾ inch cubes

1 lb Brussels sprouts, trimmed and sliced

1 garlic clove, crushed

8 scallions, cut into ½ inch slices

pinch of red pepper flakes (optional)

juice of 1 lime

2 tablespoons butter

1 avocado, sliced

½ cup cilantro leaves

salt and freshly ground black pepper

To serve

sweet chile sauce

lime wedges

quinoa, brown rice or rice noodles

The recipe is very simple and quick to make. Being a vegetarian is all about the green and making sure that you get your calories and energy, which is where the avocado comes into play. Not to mention that Brussels sprouts rock! If I were a vegetable I would be a Brussels sprout—full of nutrition and energy.

Prepare 10 minutes | **Cook** 10 minutes | **Serves** 2

1 Heat 2 tablespoons of the olive oil in a large frying pan over medium heat and fry the tofu cubes, turning as little as possible, for 2–3 minutes, or until golden and crispy. Using a spatula or slotted spoon, remove from the pan and set aside.

2 Add the Brussels sprouts to the pan along with the garlic, scallions, and chile flakes (if using). Cook for 2–3 minutes or until the Brussels sprouts are beginning to tenderize. Stir in the lime juice and butter and return the tofu to the pan. Season to taste.

3 Transfer the sprout mixture to a bowl and keep warm. Add the remaining oil to the pan along with the avocado. Cook for no more than a minute to warm through, taking care not to move the avocado around too much in the pan as it will mash. Transfer the avocado and the sprout mixture to a serving dish and scatter the cilantro leaves over the top. Drizzle with a little sweet chile sauce (if using) and a squeeze of lime and serve with quinoa, brown rice, or rice noodles.

"For me, compassion is about the stranger to whom we owe nothing. It is about how our society will be judged and how we discover our humanity. It is about finding our reward through the eyes of those to whom we owe nothing. It is about love."

Helen Bamber OBE

Piperade

2 tablespoons olive oil or butter

2 large onions, sliced

1 garlic clove, minced

3 green peppers, seeded and thinly sliced

2 red peppers, seeded and thinly sliced

1 lb tomatoes, peeled and chopped

1 teaspoon fresh oregano, chopped

1 teaspoon fresh marjoram, chopped

8 eggs, beaten

salt and freshly ground black pepper

Piperade originates from the Basque region of Spain and southern France. I love it because it is simple to make, looks good when ready to be served, and if, like me, you live in a small apartment without the benefit of a large table, it is possible to serve it to people sitting around on whatever chairs are available, or on cushions on the floor, with simply a plate and fork. I like to improvise with the vegetables depending on what's available – mushrooms work particularly well with this dish.

Prepare 15 minutes | **Cook** 25 minutes | **Serves** 4

1 Heat the olive oil or butter in a large heavy-bottomed frying pan over low heat. Add the onions and garlic and cook for 2–3 minutes or until softened. Stir in the peppers and cook for a few more minutes. Add the tomatoes, oregano, and marjoram, and season well. Stir well to combine, then cover and cook for about 15 minutes until saucy and fragrant. Season to taste.

2 Pour in the beaten eggs and cook for about 5 minutes, stirring as if cooking scrambled eggs. Remove from the heat when the eggs have just set and serve.

"If we help mothers, we help children, and, ultimately, we can rebuild whole societies."

Mariama, WfWI sponsor

Mary McCartney: Hearty pasta and bean soup

3 tablespoons olive oil
2 garlic cloves, finely chopped
2 large carrots, finely chopped
1 large onion, finely chopped
1 rib celery, trimmed and diced
14oz can cannellini or
butter beans, drained and rinsed
14oz can diced tomatoes
3 ½ cups/28oz vegetable stock
1 bay leaf
½ cup macaroni or any small
pasta
1/3 cup frozen peas
1 medium zucchini,
finely chopped (optional)
2 tablespoons chopped parsley,
½ cup Parmesan or a
vegetarian hard cheese,
finely grated (optional)
salt and freshly ground
black pepper

What I love about this soup is that it is versatile as well as tasty. It makes a great lunch as well as a first course for dinner. It can also be a substantial meal in itself, served with big crusty chunks of warm garlic bread. I find it is a good way of getting kids interested in eating beans and vegetables too!

Prepare 10 minutes | **Cook** 35 minutes | **Serves** 4

1 Heat the oil in a large pan over medium heat. Add the garlic, carrots, onion, and celery, and gently cook for 5 minutes or until softened but not colored.
2 Stir in the beans and the diced tomatoes, pour in the vegetable stock, and add the bay leaf. Bring to a boil, then reduce the heat to simmer for 20 minutes.
3 Add the pasta, peas, and zucchini (if using) and simmer for another 10 minutes, or until the pasta is cooked al dente. Stir in the parsley, season, and serve topped with grated Parmesan cheese (if using).

"We are interested in achieving things that are naturally beneficial."
Glynis Murray and Henry Braham

Trout with fennel and tarragon

½ cup fresh tarragon,
roughly chopped
½ cup sliced almonds, toasted
4 tablespoons hemp oil
2 trout, gutted and cleaned
2 fennel bulbs, sliced
salt and freshly ground
black pepper
seasonal green vegetables,
to serve

This is a homegrown recipe devised by Glyn's son, Ben. We love it because it's beautifully straightforward, and the nutty flavor of the hemp oil is perfect with the fennel and trout.

Prepare 10 minutes | **Cook** 25–30 minutes | **Serves** 2

1 Preheat the oven to 400°F. Place half the tarragon and half the sliced almonds into a small bowl. Add 2 tablespoons of the oil and mix to combine. Divide the mixture in two and stuff into the cavities of each trout.

2 Arrange the sliced fennel over the base of a roasting pan, drizzle with 1 tablespoon of the oil, and season. Place the stuffed fish on top of the fennel and drizzle with the remaining oil. Bake for 25–30 minutes, or until the trout are cooked and will flake off the bones. Scatter the remaining toasted almonds and tarragon over the top, and serve with seasonal green vegetables.

"Women have a natural inherent knowingness, an unspoken connection between us, as mothers, wives, and sisters."

Robin Wright

Lettuce wraps

4 boston lettuces

4 tablespoons honey

2 tablespoons soy sauce

1 garlic clove, finely chopped

1-inch piece fresh ginger, peeled and grated

1 tablespoon sesame seeds

1 tablespoon sesame oil

1 cup walnuts, pecans, or hazelnuts

½ cup celery, diced

½ cup carrots, diced

½ cup red pepper, diced

¼ cup scallions, chopped

½ cup fresh cilantro, chopped

½–1 red chile, chopped

salt and freshly ground black pepper

For the garnish

½ cup bean sprouts

1 carrot, grated

fresh cilantro leaves

For the sweet chile sauce

1–2 tablespoons red chiles, finely chopped

¾ cup sugar

1 cup rice vinegar

2 garlic cloves, finely chopped

1-inch piece of ginger, peeled and finely chopped

1 teaspoon salt

A vegetarian version of a traditional Thai appetizer called *larb nua*, this recipe was inspired by Diana Stobo's amazing raw food dishes. It's a light and refreshing snack, reminiscent of a spring roll. I particularly love the sauce, which gives the dish an authentic Thai taste.

Prepare 15 minutes | **Serves** 4 as a main (6 as a starter)

1 Carefully pull the lettuce leaves apart to produce about 20 whole leaves. Wash thoroughly, dry with paper towels, and trim the stem ends.

2 Place the honey, soy sauce, garlic, ginger, sesame seeds, and sesame oil into a food processor or blender and process to combine. Add the nuts, vegetables, cilantro and chile to the processor and process until evenly chopped.

3 Arrange 2–3 lettuce leaves on a plate and scoop 2–3 tablespoons of nut mixture into each leaf. Garnish with the bean sprouts, grated carrot, and a few cilantro leaves, and serve with Sweet chile sauce (see below).

Sweet chile sauce

Prepare 5 minutes | **Cook** 20 minutes | **Serves** 4

1 Put the chiles, sugar, and rice vinegar into a small, heavy-bottomed saucepan. Cook over low heat, stirring, until the sugar dissolves. Bring to a boil and immediately reduce the heat to simmer.

2 Add the garlic and ginger and cook for 15–20 minutes until the chiles are soft. Season to taste with salt.

3 Process with a stick blender until smooth, season with salt, to taste, and serve with the lettuce wraps.

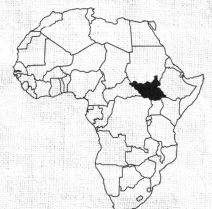

SOUTH SUDAN

Average WfWI participant

Age: 31-40

Married: 84% / Widowed: 16%

Children: 4 / No. in household: 11

Literate: 4% / No formal education: 95%

Matida's Story

In the spring of 2008, Women for Women International launched its first agribusiness initiative. Over the course of its first three years, the program trained more than 3,000 women how to use sustainable farming practices to grow crops that can be sold for profit in the local market, as well as feed their families. On average, women like Matida are making twice the average per capita income in South Sudan. The farm has also contributed to restoring community in a region that has been riven with tribal violence in the last decade.

"I grew up in a cattle camp where soldiers would stop to rest before returning to the battlefront. Girls in my camp had to carry the soldiers' luggage and ammunition to the next station. Sometimes the soldiers would also 'ask' us to sleep with them. There was no way to refuse.

Our home was burned by a militia, and we fled to Ethiopia. The refugee camp there was a town of tents sunk in the mud. There were beds for a lucky few, but most of us slept on the ground at night, and some slept standing up. Those with beds traded places with us—there were many kindnesses like this. We were surrounded by barbed wire and felt like we were in a cage. We tried to write to people. We wrote to government officials, UN officials, we wrote to NGOs, we wrote to whoever we knew, hoping that someone, anyone, would come, see what we were going through, and save us from this hell.

I have had much darkness but also much light in my life. After returning to my country, I met my husband Bakri and we now have three children, including our new baby Matak. I began working on the farm when it opened in 2008, cultivating six plots of kale, black-eyed peas, and okra. From these crops I now earn as much as 50 South Sudanese pounds per day-almost enough to support my family. In my Dinka community, most men take many wives, but I am Bakri's only wife, and we love each other very much. When I cannot tend to the farm, he does it for me, and when I must work, he looks after our little boy. My prayers have been answered."

SOUTH SUDAN

Population: 10,625,176

Square km: 644,329

GDP per capita: $2,700

Conflict dates: 1983-present

Total no. killed: 300,000-2.7 million
(estimated in North & South Sudan)

Internally displaced persons: 560,161

Recipes from South Sudan

Sudanese food, although obviously African, has also been much influenced by the Arab traders and settlers who arrived during the Ottoman Empire introducing ingredients such as garlic and red pepper as well as dishes such as meatballs and pastries. Although not always readily available, tomatoes, cabbage (*sucamawiki*), and okra are all popular.

Sudanese people like to eat meals around a communal tray where meat, vegetables, salad, and sauces are all placed together. Food is eaten with the right hand, using flatbread or a type of firm porridge called *aseeda* (made from either wheat flour or corn to which dates and milk are sometimes added) to scoop up the food from the tray. With a greater number of lakes and swamps than in the north of the country, the South Sudanese people are more dependent on fish for their food. A popular stew from this area is *kajaik*, which is made from dried fish. Elsewhere, *kawari*, a soup made from cattle or sheep's hooves, as well as vegetables and spices, is a staple.

Salata aswad de zabadi

A vegetable salad of eggplant and peppers tossed in a peanut yogurt dressing and served cooled with flatbreads.

Prepare 20 minutes | **Cook** 20–25 minutes | **Serves** 6

8 tablespoons vegetable oil
4 large eggplants, cut into 1-inch pieces
1 tablespoon tomato paste
²/₃ cup plain yogurt
2 tablespoons peanut butter
juice of 2 lemons
2 green peppers, deseeded and roughly chopped
2 large tomatoes, roughly chopped
2 garlic cloves, peeled and finely chopped
Salt and freshly ground black pepper
flatbreads, to serve

1 Heat 2 tablespoons of the vegetable oil in a large frying pan, and fry the eggplant in batches, adding more oil as needed, for about 10 minutes or until soft. Set aside to cool.
2 In a large bowl, mix together the tomato paste, yogurt, and peanut butter. Season generously with salt and black pepper. Stir in the lemon juice, and add the green peppers, tomatoes, and garlic. Mix in the cooled eggplant and serve with flatbreads.

Baseema

Baseema means "delicious," and this soft, sweet, cakey biscuit certainly lives up to its name.

Prepare 15 minutes | **Cook** 40 minutes | **Serves** 10–12

5 eggs
1 cup confectioners sugar
³/₄ cup vegetable oil
2 cups plain yogurt
2 teaspoons vanilla extract
2½ cups all-purpose flour
2 teaspoons baking powder
½ cup dried coconut

For the syrup
1 ³/₄ cups sugar
1 tablespoon lemon juice

1 Preheat the oven to 350° F. Grease and line a 9 × 12 inch baking pan with nonstick parchment paper. Beat the eggs and confectioners sugar together until light and frothy. Add the oil, yogurt and vanilla extract and stir gently.
2 In a separate bowl, sift the flour with the baking powder and stir in the coconut. Then fold this into the egg and yogurt mixture. Pour this mixture into the prepared baking pan and bake for 30–35 minutes.
2 Place the sugar, lemon juice, and 1 cup of water in a small pan. Slowly bring to a boil and boil for 5 minutes until the syrup thickens. Pour over the cake while it is still warm, and leave to soak in before serving.

"There is nothing better than putting a plate of delicious food on the table for the people you love."
Alice Waters

Lentil salad

1 cup green lentils, washed
1–2 tablespoons red wine vinegar
3 tablespoons extra virgin olive oil
2 shallots, thinly sliced
3 scallions, finely chopped
3 tablespoons chopped
fresh parsley or cilantro,
plus extra to serve
1 tablespoon olive oil
8oz peeled raw shrimp
salt and freshly ground
black pepper

I love to make this lentil salad as a nourishing lunch or as an accompaniment to dinner. There are so many different possibilities and variations with this recipe — the salad can reflect any season beautifully.

Prepare 5 minutes | **Cook** 40 minutes | **Serves** 4

1 Place the lentils in a pan and cover with cold water by 2–3 inches. Bring to a boil, then reduce the heat to a simmer and cook for about 30 minutes (adding more water if necessary) until the lentils are tender. Drain and reserve ½ cup of the cooking liquid.

2 Toss the warm cooked lentils with 1 tablespoon of the red wine vinegar and season with a little salt and freshly ground black pepper. Leave to stand for 5 minutes, then taste and add more salt and/or red wine vinegar, if needed. Add the extra virgin olive oil, shallots, and scallions and mix well. Stir in the chopped parsley or cilantro. If the lentils seem dry and are hard to stir, loosen them with a little of the reserved cooking liquid.

3 Heat the olive oil in a pan and cook the shrimp for 4–5 minutes until they are pink and opaque. Serve with the lentil salad, scattered with some chopped parsley or cilantro.

Cook's tip

This recipe is extremely versatile; try the following variations (omitting the prawns):
• Add half a diced cucumber to the cooked lentils.
• Finely dice a small carrot, half a celery rib, and an onion, and cook in
   1–2 tablespoons olive oil until tender. Allow to cool before adding to the lentils
   in place of the shallot and scallions.
• Garnish with ½ cup crumbled feta or goat cheese.
• Add ½ teaspoon toasted and crushed cumin seeds.
• Sprinkle ¼ diced red pepper with salt. Leave to stand for 5 minutes to soften,
   then stir in with the shallots and scallions.

"I have learned from WfWI that I have the right to choose who leads me."
Roseline, WfWI Nigeria participant

Trudie Styler: Spaghetti al aglio e olio

1 lb dried spaghetti

³/₄–1 cup extra virgin olive oil

6–8 garlic cloves, chopped

1½ teaspoons red pepper flakes

finely grated or shaved Parmesan cheese, to serve

salt and freshly ground black pepper

I absolutely love Italy, and Sting and I spend as much time as we can at our home in Tuscany. This pasta dish is classic Italian simplicity. The flavors of fine olive oil, garlic, and spicy red pepper flakes combine perfectly to create the ultimate comfort food with a kick that keeps you coming back for more. A generous shaving of good Parmesan completes the dish, and all in about 10 minutes flat. A delicious quick lunch or simple supper that anyone can make—equally scrumptious with gluten-free pasta, quinoa, or rice spaghetti.

Prepare 5 minutes | **Cook** 10 minutes | **Serves** 4–6

1 Cook the pasta in a large pot of boiling salted water for about 8–10 minutes or until barely tender but firm to the bite. Drain and reserve about 4 tablespoons of the cooking water. Set aside and keep warm.

2 Return the pan to medium heat and pour in the extra virgin olive oil. Add the garlic and red pepper flakes, then reduce the heat and immediately add the drained hot pasta and the reserved cooking water. Toss and stir so that the oil and water emulsify. Serve immediately, topped with grated Parmesan and accompanied by a bitter leaf salad (see below).

Cook's tip Pasta cooking water is the secret ingredient of this dish. It has a unique flavor, a combination of the salt and high starch content.

Bitter leaf salad with an olive oil, citrus, and caper dressing

1 fennel bulb

1 radicchio

3 cups/4oz watercress

2 cup/2oz wild arugula

2 tablespoons capers

2 tablespoons olive oil

juice of 1 lemon

juice of 1 orange

2 tablespoons grated or shaved Parmesan or Pecorino cheese (optional)

salt and freshly ground black pepper

Prepare 5 minutes | **Serves** 4

1 Finely slice the fennel and radicchio and place in a large bowl with the watercress, arugula, and capers.

2 In a small bowl, mix together the olive oil and the lemon and orange juices. Pour the dressing over the salad and sprinkle with the cheese (if using). Season with a little salt (not too much since the capers and cheese are salty) and lots of freshly ground black pepper.

"What inspires me is seeing the strength of the women in the DRC, who despite often being subjected to the cruellest assaults are still able to stay strong for their families. They deserve our support and I'll keep running to make more people aware of what they have been through and how people can help them."

Chris Jackson

Marathon chicken pesto pasta

3 tablespoons extra virgin olive oil

2 chicken breasts, cut into thin strips

12oz dried pasta, such as penne, fusilli, or rigatoni

1 head broccoli cut into tiny florets

1 cup heavy cream

For the pesto

4 cups/4oz basil leaves

3 tablespoons pine nuts, toasted

3–4 garlic cloves

$^1/_3$ cup Parmesan or Grana Padano, grated, plus shavings to serve

1–2 tablespoons lemon juice

$^2/_3$ cup extra virgin olive oil

salt and freshly ground black pepper

In 2010 I decided to run 12 marathons in 12 months, including one in the Democratic Republic of Congo, to raise awareness about the situation there and the work that WfWI does in the region. Although I loved eating sugar cane while running in the DRC, and on the morning of the marathon had a simple omelet, I became increasingly aware during the challenge of the importance of eating the right meal before a race. To enable me to reach the finish line in the fastest time, I developed this tasty recipe, which is packed full of energy and helps me run to the best of my ability.

Prepare 20 minutes | **Cook** 10 minutes | **Serves** 4 (or 2 marathon portions)

1 First make the pesto. Place all of the ingredients, except the olive oil, in a blender or food processor and process to combine. Add enough of the olive oil to form a smooth but slightly chunky paste and process until smooth.

2 Now for the chicken. Mix 2 tablespoons of the pesto with 1–2 tablespoons of the extra virgin olive oil and smear over the chicken strips. Place in a dish, cover, and leave to marinate in the fridge for at least 15 minutes. Meanwhile, cook the pasta in a large pan of salted boiling water until al dente.

3 Heat a little of the olive oil in a frying or grill pan and cook the chicken, in batches, for about 5 minutes until golden and crispy and thoroughly cooked through. Add the broccoli to the pasta pan for the final 2 minutes of the pasta cooking time.

4 Once the pasta and broccoli are cooked, drain thoroughly and return to the pan over medium heat. Season with freshly ground black pepper and stir in the cooked chicken and broccoli. Stir in the remaining pesto and the cream. Cook for another minute. Serve with shavings of Parmesan or Grana Padano accompanied by a crisp green salad, a slice of garlic bread, and a large glass of water to keep hydrated.

"Now I can imagine a tomorrow that could be better than today."
Elizabeth, WfWI Rwanda participant

"There has to be increased awareness of the fact that the food choices each of us makes have a knock-on global effect. I see it as very much a part of my job to talk about these issues."

Allegra McEvedy

Barley bits salad with honeyed goat cheese toast

½ cup pearl barley or pearled spelt

2 cups cold vegetable or light chicken stock (make it half strength if using a cube)

2 garlic cloves, finely chopped and mashed with salt to make a paste

1 lb any quick-cook vegetables, cut into small pieces

4oz goat cheese

4 slices bread

2 teaspoons honey

1 lemon

$^1/_4$ cup extra virgin olive oil

½ cup fresh herbs (parsley, basil, chives, mint, or dill), chopped

The joy of this salad is that it's a proper vegetable drawer clear-out of all the quick-cook stuff, as opposed to the roots. We all end up with half a bag of snow peas or sugar snaps, a quarter of a cabbage, an ear of corn, and a stray zucchini in our fridge, and the beauty of this filling salad is that it uses any stray odds and ends without looking like it. Green beans, fennel, asparagus, peas, and cucumber all work fine, too, but leave asparagus tips whole. I'm relying on your having a few fresh herbs around, too. Wilting parsley or dill—doesn't matter (although cilantro doesn't work so well), this dish indiscriminately uses whatever you have, bound with barley and lifted by the delicious toasts that are the real superstar.

Prepare 20 minutes | **Cook** 45 minutes | **Serves** 4–6

1 Place the barley or spelt into a large pan, pour in the cold stock, and bring to a boil over medium heat, then simmer gently for about half an hour. When you can see the barley or spelt through the liquid, put a lid on it and turn the heat right down—the idea is that the barley or spelt absorbs all the flavor of the stock. (If the barley or spelt is cooked but there is still some liquid left, boil it hard for a few minutes until it's all gone, taking care not to let it stick on the bottom.) Once the barley is cooked, stir in half of the garlic paste, then season well and spread out on a plate to cool.

2 Rinse out the pan, fill with salted water, and bring to a rolling boil. Add all your vegetables, cover, and prepare a bowl of very cold water, preferably iced. As soon as the pan comes back to a boil, strain the vegetables and pour them into the cold water (this keeps them green and stops them cooking, which is essential for this super-fresh and crunchy salad). Once the vegetables are cool, drain.

3 Preheat the oven to 350°F. Divide the goat cheese among the 4 slices of bread, then drizzle with the honey—about $^1/_2$ teaspoon on each. Lay the bread on a foil-lined baking sheet and bake them in the oven for about 12–15 minutes. The toasts will smell fantastic when they are ready as the cheese will have melted and the honey caramelized.

4 Rustle up the dressing with the juice of half the lemon. Whisk in the olive oil, stir in the remaining garlic paste, and finish with the chopped herbs. In a big bowl, mix together the barley and vegetables with the dressing and some salt and pepper, then taste. You want this one to be dressed pretty sharply to play with the honey. Cut the remaining lemon half into wedges and serve the salad with these and the goat cheese toasts.

"I believe it is vital to transform the world by changing the way people treat each other, and by modelling that kind of changed behavior ourselves."

Anne Firth Murray

Fruit and nut oaty bars

10 tablespoons unsalted butter, cut into cubes

$^1/_3$ cup brown sugar

3 tablespoons honey

1 $^2/_3$ cups oats

1 cup dried fruit such as dried cherries, dried cranberries, or raisins

½ cup hazelnuts, toasted and chopped

These delicious bars are full of energy-boosting oats, honey, juicy dried fruit, and nuts. A perfect mid-morning pick-me-up.

Prepare 5 minutes | **Cook** 25 minutes | **Makes** 12

1 Preheat the oven to 350°F. Place the butter, sugar, and honey in a medium pan over low heat and heat gently, stirring occasionally, until the butter has melted and the sugar has dissolved.

2 Remove from the heat and stir in the oats, dried fruit, and nuts. Press the mixture into a lightly greased 8 × 12 × 2 inch rectangular nonstick roasting pan and bake in the oven for 20–25 minutes, until golden brown.

3 Allow to cool in the pan for 5 minutes, then score lightly with a knife into 12 bars. Leave to cool completely in the pan before removing. The bars can be stored in an airtight container for up to 4 days.

Cook's tip

For a change of flavor, try replacing the dried cherries, dried cranberries, or raisins with an equal amount of chopped dried apricots or dates.

> "WfWI helped me learn how, when you make a small step, you make a small breakthrough. Over time, you begin to see things differently, and get your will for life back."
>
> **Ahida, WfWI Bosnia and Herzegovina participant**

Nell Newman: Orange scented olive oil almond cake

¾ cup almonds (or ¾ cup almond flour)
¾ cup rice flour
¼ teaspoon baking powder
½ teaspoon salt
3 large eggs, separated
¾ cup sugar
½ cup olive oil
2 teaspoons vanilla extract
½ teaspoon almond extract
freshly grated zest of 2 oranges and ½ cup juice, plus orange segments to decorate (optional)
¼ cup cooking sherry or Sauternes

To serve
almond flakes (optional)
slightly sweetened whipped cream or crème fraîche
fresh berries

This cake is delicious served as it comes with tea or coffee, but is even better accompanied by slightly sweetened whipped cream and berries. Using rice flour makes it gluten free, but you'd never know it. I always use organic ingredients in my cooking, and for this recipe I use our Newman's Own Organics Olive Oil. Do be sure to use a light, fruity organic olive oil, as a heavy one won't work. Enjoy!

Prepare 15 minutes | **Cook** 40 minutes | **Serves** 8

1 Preheat the oven to 350°F. Grease an 8-inch round cake or spring-form pan, and line the base with parchment paper.

2 Toast the almonds in a frying pan over medium heat until lightly browned. Cool, then grind in a food processor until fine. Sift out the big pieces and measure out ¾ cup. Alternatively, use almond flour.

3 In a mixing bowl, sift together the rice flour and ground almonds with the baking powder and salt.

4 Meanwhile, in a separate large mixing bowl, beat the egg yolks with an electric whisk until they are light in color and texture, about 1 minute. Add the sugar and beat for a further 2–3 minutes until well combined. Continue to whisk and add the olive oil in a slow stream, followed by the vanilla and almond extracts, grated orange zest, orange juice and the sherry or Sauternes. Then fold the dry ingredients into this mixture, until just combined.

5 Whisk the egg whites in a clean bowl using the electric whisk (make sure the beaters are clean) until firm peaks form. Fold the egg whites into the yolk/flour mixture until well combined—I prefer to use a clean hand for this, but you may use a spoon if you wish. Pour the batter into the prepared cake pan.

6 Bake in the oven for 30–40 minutes until light brown and a toothpick inserted into the middle comes out clean.

7 When the cake is cooked, allow to cool in its pan for about 15 minutes, then run a butter knife around the edges of the pan before carefully inverting onto a clean, folded tea towel. Remove the paper from the base and invert onto a cooling rack (this prevents the rack leaving marks on the top of the cake). Garnish with flaked almonds and serve plain or with cream or crème fraîche and berries.

WOMEN *for* WOMEN
International

nurture

nutritious family recipes

"I can't imagine, as a mother, what it would be like to watch a child die.
As a UNICEF ambassador, I know that it's the children under five who die first."

Mia Farrow

Breakfast pancakes

1 cup wholewheat flour
¼ cup instant dry milk (optional)
1 tablespoon sugar
1 teaspoon baking powder
³/₄ teaspoon baking soda
2 eggs, beaten
1 tablespoon vegetable oil
or melted butter, plus extra
for frying
1 tablespoon applesauce
²/₃ cup milk

Pancake extras (optional)
½ banana, mashed
some blueberries
pinch of ground cinnamon

To serve
maple syrup or honey,
plain yogurt, and fruit

Prepare 5 minutes | **Cook** 20 minutes | **Makes** 9–10

1 In a large bowl, mix together the flour and the dry milk, sugar, baking powder, and baking soda. Make a well in the center. Pour in the beaten eggs and the oil or melted butter, add the applesauce, and start mixing together. Gradually stir in the milk until the batter is of a dropping consistency. Stir in the extras of your choice, if you are adding them.

2 Heat a little oil or melted butter in a large nonstick frying pan. Drop a large table-spoon of the batter per pancake into the pan. Cooking in batches of 2–3, cook for 3 minutes over medium heat until small bubbles appear on the surface. Turn and cook the other side for 2–3 minutes or until golden. Remove from the pan and keep warm, covered, while you continue cooking with the remaining batter. Serve drizzled with maple syrup or honey, or yogurt and fruit, or a topping of your choice.

"I believe in and have seen the resilience and power of children, in spite of all the terrible experiences they have been through. In my work with former child soldiers, I see valuable knowledge and potential, which gives me great hope."

Marco Borsato

Individual carrot cakes

1¼ cups brown sugar
1 cup vegetable or sunflower oil
3 eggs, beaten
2½ cups self-rising flour
2 teaspoons pumpkin pie spice
1 lb carrots, peeled and finely grated
Finely grated zest of 1 orange
1¾ cups walnuts, chopped
1 ½ cups raisins

For the frosting
1½ cups confectioners sugar
7oz cream cheese
1–1½ tablespoons orange juice
finely grated zest of 1 orange

Prepare 15 minutes | **Cook** 30 minutes | **Makes** 12

1 Preheat the oven to 350°F. Grease and flour the sides of a large muffin pan and place a disk of parchment paper at the base of each cup. Place on a large baking sheet.

2 In a large bowl, beat together the sugar and oil for 2–3 minutes, before adding the eggs and mixing well. Sift the flour and pumpkin pie spice into the bowl and mix well.

3 Stir in the carrot, orange zest, walnuts, and raisins until just combined. Spoon the mixture evenly in the muffin cups and bake in the oven for 25–30 minutes, or until a toothpick placed in the center comes out clean. Turn the cakes out onto a rack and allow to cool.

3 Meanwhile, make the frosting. Sift the confectioners sugar into a bowl, add the cream cheese, and beat until combined. Gradually add the orange juice until the mixture is of a spreadable consistency. Spread evenly over the tops of each carrot cake, sprinkle with the orange zest, and serve.

BOSNIA and HERZEGOVINA

Average WfWI participant

Age: 31-40

Married: 73% / Widowed: 12% / Single: 15%

Children: 2

Literate: 92% / No formal education: 10%

Miloska's story

Although the war in Bosnia and Herzegovina ended in 1995, its catastrophic effect on the economy is still being felt today. It shattered lives, and women there continue to struggle to heal wounds and rebuild communities. It was here, in 1993, that Zainab Salbi felt compelled to start Women for Women International, after she and her husband witnessed the devastation that the war had caused. Since then, 351,000 women have been served in Bosnia and Herzegovina.

"When the Serbs came, we fled Srebrenica. The last memory I have of my home was looking at my sons under a tree in the front garden. My husband and boys ran into the woods and up into the mountains, and my daughter-in-law and I ran in the other direction. She and I survived; they didn't. My sons were only 22 and 16 years old. The elder one was about to become a father. They haven't found the bodies of either of them yet, or that of my husband—I hope that one day I will be able to bury them.

I came back to Srebrenica in 2000, to walk where my sons last walked. I had police protection, but just before we got to my house they told me that they would not go in with me and that if I went any farther it was at my own risk. A Serb family was living there, and when I knocked they did not open the door, though I knew they were in. I was not scared. I just wanted to see if there were any photos left of my family. Someone finally answered—they told me to go away and threatened to kill me if I came back, but they didn't frighten me. In my mind I saw my sons standing there next to the tree where I had last seen them.

Then I found out about Women for Women International. Thanks to their microcredit program, I was able to get a loan and build a house for myself and my grandchildren. Through the skills training they offered, I also learned about growing vegetables and rearing chickens, which I sell in the market. Just as importantly I met my friends, whose support is so vital to me: we understand each other.

Through the worst, I never lost hope that life would get better and was inspired by words from a Bosnian song, "There is always enough space in the top when you start from the bottom." And so I realized that my life couldn't get any worse, it could only get better, because I was starting from the bottom."

BOSNIA and HERZEGOVINA

Population: 3,879,296

Square km: 51,197

GDP per capita: $8,100

Unemployment: 47%

Life expectancy:
Female: 82 years / Male: 75 years

Conflict dates: 1992-1995

Total no. killed: 97,210+

Estimated military deaths: 57,520+

Estimated civilian deaths: 39,685+

Internally displaced persons: 113,000

Recipe from Bosnia and Herzegovina

Bosnia and Herzegovina's cuisine has been influenced by that of the Turks and also their other Eastern European neighbors. It makes use of many spices but in moderate quantities. Dishes tend to be light, and meat-usually beef or lamb-is often cooked in a sealed pot with vegetables, resulting in flavorsome sauces. Tomatoes, onions, garlic, peppers, potatoes, cucumbers, carrots, cabbages, and mushrooms are all grown widely and so frequently feature on Bosnian tables. Breakfast often consists of cheese, in particular *travnički*, a sharp cheese made from sheep's milk. Lunch, traditionally the main meal of the day, may include bread, soups, stews, kebabs, ground meat sausages (*cevapcici*), stuffed cabbage or grape leaves (*dolma* and *sarma*), and stuffed peppers. Bosnia has its own version of the honey pastry baklava, but other desserts usually have fresh fruit and cream as the main ingredients. Rakija, a local brandy produced with apples or plums, is typically Bosnian, while local wines come from Herzegovina, where the climate is suitable for grape growing and wine making.

Baklava

Sweet, sticky, crisp layers of pastry sandwiching a walnut filling, all drenched in a spiced syrup.

Prepare 1 hour | **Cook** 45 minutes | **Makes** 24

2 cinnamon sticks
6 whole cloves
3 whole black peppercorns
3½ cups walnuts, finely chopped
finely grated zest of 1 lemon
6 tablespoons sugar
16 sheets phyllo pastry
vegetable oil, to grease tin
5-6 tablespoons unsalted butter, melted

For the syrup
2¼ cups sugar
pinch of sea salt flakes
juice of 1 lemon and 3 strips zest, 2 inches each
3 strips orange zest, 2 inches each
1 cinnamon stick, broken

1 Preheat the oven to 400°F. Put the spices and peppercorns in a dry pan and roast over high heat for 2 minutes until you start to smell the aromas. Allow to cool, then place in a spice grinder, or mortar and pestle, and grind finely. Place the walnuts in a bowl and add the ground spice mixture with the lemon zest and sugar. Set aside.

2 Open out the phyllo pastry, and cover with a damp towel to prevent it from drying out. Brush a rectangular baking pan, about 7 × 12 inches and 1-2 inches deep, with vegetable oil. Brush a sheet of phyllo with melted butter and place in the baking pan. Repeat to make 8 layers. Trim to a snug fit.

3 Add the nut mixture and spread evenly. Brush the remaining pastry with butter and layer until all the pastry is used. Trim the top to a snug fit. Press down gently with the palm of your hand. Lightly score the pastry top but do not cut all the way through into the nuts. Criss-cross in diagonal lines, 2 inches apart, to make a diamond pattern. Brush the top with butter and bake in the oven for 25-30 minutes.

4 Meanwhile, make the syrup. Put the sugar in a pan with 1¼ cups water, the sea salt flakes, lemon juice, strips of lemon and orange zest, and the cinnamon. Heat gently until the sugar dissolves. Bring to a boil and boil for 5-8 minutes until the syrup is light and slightly thickened. Cool quickly by placing the pan in a bowl of ice.

5 Remove the baklava from the oven. Cut the pastry all the way through to make at least 24 pieces. Remove and discard the cinnamon stick and citrus zest, then gently spoon the syrup over the baklava. Cool completely and serve.

"I was inspired to start FEED after traveling around the world and seeing firsthand how so many do not have enough food to sustain themselves and their families. I believe it is our obligation to help those who are hungry and living in dire poverty around the world."

Lauren Bush Lauren

Butternut squash soup

2 tablespoons olive oil
2 tablespoons butter
1 onion, chopped
1 celery rib, chopped
2 garlic cloves, crushed
1-inch piece of fresh ginger, peeled and grated
1 butternut squash, about 2 lbs, peeled, seeded and chopped into 1-inch chunks
4 cups vegetable stock
2–3 sprigs fresh thyme
4 tablespoons cider, or to taste (optional)
handful of pumpkin seeds, toasted
salt and freshly ground black pepper

For the cornbread
¾ cup all-purpose flour
1 tablespoon baking powder
¼ teaspoon salt
²/₃ cup cornmeal
²/₃ cup Cheddar cheese, finely grated
pinch of red pepper flakes
2 eggs, beaten
1¼ cups milk
4 tablespoons butter, melted, plus extra to grease

This is a personal favorite of mine! It evokes memories of cozy autumn days, and it is quick and easy to make.

Prepare 10 minutes | **Cook** 40 minutes | **Serves** 4–6

1 Heat the oil and butter in a large pan over medium heat and gently cook the onion, celery, garlic and ginger for about 5 minutes or until softened. Stir in the squash and cook, covered, for another 10–15 minutes.

2 Pour in the vegetable stock, add the thyme sprigs and season. Bring to a boil and simmer for about 20 minutes, or until the squash is very soft and tender. Add a little cider to taste, if liked.

3 Blitz the soup in a food processor or blender in batches until completely smooth. Adjust the seasoning to taste, scatter over the pumpkin seeds and serve with a seeded bread, or try my Cornbread (see below).

Corn bread

Prepare 20 minutes | **Cook** 45 minutes | **Makes** 6–8 slices

1 Preheat the oven to 400°F. Grease and line a 32oz loaf pan. Place the flour, baking powder, salt, and cornmeal into a large mixing bowl, add the cheese and red pepper flakes, then mix well (use your fingertips to make sure the cheese is evenly distributed).

2 Make a well in the center and pour in the beaten eggs, milk, and melted butter. Stir with a wooden spoon until smooth.

3 Pour the mixture into the loaf pan and bake for 40–45 minutes until risen and golden brown, and firm to the touch.

4 Leave to cool in the pan for 10 minutes before turning out onto a cooling rack. Serve warm or cold, cut into slices.

"I fell in love with cooking in my teens, and I often say it saved my life. In the third decade of my cooking career, I realized that one of the most important things about food was giving back."

Ann Cooper

Fresh sweetcorn chowder

1 teaspoon olive oil
½ cup onions, chopped
1 garlic clove, finely chopped
½ teaspoon ground cumin
3 cups fresh corn kernels
(from about 5 cobs)
1 lb potatoes, peeled and diced
4 cups vegetable stock
¾ cup milk
1 teaspoon fresh cilantro,
chopped
salt and freshly ground
black pepper

Living in the Southwest of America has helped me fall in love with late summer produce such as corn. This chowder recipe utilizes traditional Southwest flavours, highlighting the corn's natural sweet creaminess, and makes a great addition to any late summer or early autumn meal.

Prepare 10 minutes | **Cook** 30 minutes | **Serves** 4

1 Heat the oil in a large pan over a medium heat and fry the onions for about 5 minutes or until softened. Add the garlic and cumin and cook for a further minute.
2 Stir in the corn kernels and potatoes, then season well. Pour in the stock, bring to the boil, then reduce the heat to a simmer. Cook for 20–30 minutes or until the potatoes are softened.
3 Stir in the milk and cilantro, return to the heat to heat through, then serve with a fresh garden salad or crusty bread.

Cook's tip

If the flavor of cilantro is too strong for your liking, try replacing it with parsley or another of your favorite garden herbs.

Spicy cashew tomato soup

8oz cashew nuts

14oz can peeled plum tomatoes

1 teaspoon cumin seeds

1 teaspoon fennel seeds

1 teaspoon coriander seeds

1 tablespoon olive oil

1 red onion, chopped

3 celery ribs, chopped

2 garlic cloves, crushed

½–1 teaspoon cayenne pepper, to taste

juice of 1 lime or half a lemon, to taste

½ cucumber, peeled, seeded, and diced

chopped cilantro leaves, to garnish

salt and freshly ground black pepper

This soup, which my Zen teacher Edward Brown taught me how to make, is great for a relaxing dinner party with friends.

Prepare 10 minutes | **Cook** 25 minutes | **Serves** 4

1 Place the cashew nuts into a large bowl and pour in 3 cups cold water. Blend using a stick blender, then add the tomatoes and blend again until smooth. Grind the cumin, fennel, and coriander seeds to a powder using a mortar and pestle or a spice grinder.

2 Heat the oil in a large pan and cook the onion for 2–3 minutes or until beginning to soften, then add the celery and continue cooking for another 2–3 minutes. When the celery has softened, add the garlic, cayenne pepper, and ground spices. Cook for a minute or two before adding the tomato and cashew nut mixture. Simmer for 10–15 minutes, stirring occasionally to avoid burning the cashews on the bottom of the pan.

3 Add the lime or lemon juice and season with salt to taste. Serve scattered with the diced cucumber and chopped cilantro leaves.

Cook's tip

Make the soup more substantial by adding 10oz raw shrimp when adding the tomato and cashew nut mixture to the pan in step 2. You could also use almonds as an alternative to the cashew nuts.

"As both a mother of five and a campaigner for global access to medicine and vaccines, I have seen firsthand how populations suffer when inequity triumphs and how vaccines can have an enormous, positive impact on future generations."

Alisa Swidler

Quorn and pepper tacos

2 tablespoons olive oil

2 lbs frozen ground quorn

4 × 14oz cans kidney beans, drained and rinsed

2 garlic cloves, crushed

4 teaspoons paprika

2 teaspoons dried red pepper flakes

2 teaspoons cayenne pepper

24 corn taco shells

salt and freshly ground black pepper

Accompaniments

4 red peppers, seeded and thinly sliced

4 yellow peppers, seeded and thinly sliced

2 cups Cheddar cheese, grated

1 Iceberg lettuce, shredded

4 large tomatoes, chopped

1 red onion, sliced

3 ripe avocados, sliced

4 limes, cut into wedges

few handfuls of cilantro leaves

With five kids who disagree about all food other than dessert, this recipe is a winner every time—who doesn't like taco night? Even their non-vegetarian friends are converts. The real key is heating those taco shells!

Prepare 15 minutes | **Cook** 25 minutes | **Makes** 24

1 Preheat the oven to 350°F. Heat 1 tablespoon of the oil in a large frying pan over medium heat. Add the frozen quorn, the kidney beans, the garlic, and all of the spices. Stir in $1/2$ cup water. Cover and gently simmer for about 20 minutes, or until the mixture is cooked through, but not overcooked and mushy. Season to taste.

2 Meanwhile, heat the remaining oil in a separate pan and cook the peppers, in batches, for 3–4 minutes or until softened, then place in a serving bowl. Arrange the other accompaniments in individual bowls or on plates.

3 Warm the taco shells in the oven for 6 minutes. The best way is to stand them on their rounded edges on a baking sheet so they won't fall over.

4 Serve the ground quorn mix with all the accompaniments for everyone to fill their taco as they wish.

Cook's tip

Chickpeas are a great addition to the tacos and provide extra protein. Simply drain and rinse a can or two and add in step 1, 10 minutes before the end of the cooking time. You could try melting the cheese in the taco shells before serving, and perhaps offer hot pepper sauce for adults or sour cream for kids.

"Our generation has inherited an incredibly beautiful world. It is in our hands whether our children and their children inherit the same world. When you have conflict, everything else breaks down... so the absolute key is to try to get these conflicts resolved."

Sir Richard Branson and family

Spaghetti bolognese

1 teaspoon vegetable oil
1 onion, chopped
3 garlic cloves, finely chopped
2lbs ground beef
2 carrots, finely grated
14oz can chopped tomatoes
3 tablespoons tomato paste
²/₃ cup red wine
²/₃ cup beef stock
1 lb spaghetti
grated Parmesan cheese, to serve

Prepare 10 minutes | **Cook** 45 minutes | **Serves** 4-6

1 Heat the oil in a large pan over medium heat, add the onion and cook gently for 5–6 minutes, or until softened. Add the garlic and cook for another minute. Stir in the ground beef and cook, stirring continuously, for 5 minutes or until browned.

2 Add the grated carrots, tomatoes, and tomato paste. Pour in the red wine and beef stock. Mix thoroughly, cover, and bring to a boil, then reduce the heat and simmer for 20 minutes, adding a little water if needed.

3 Meanwhile, cook the spaghetti in a large pan of boiling salted water for about 10 minutes, or until the pasta is al dente. Drain the spaghetti and serve the bolognese sauce either stirred through the spaghetti or spooned over the top, sprinkled with grated Parmesan.

Cook's tip

You can use the bolognese sauce as the base for a cottage pie. Pour the mixture into a shallow baking dish and cover with cooked potatoes mashed with milk, butter, and grated Cheddar cheese. Bake at 350°F for 20–25 minutes or until the potato topping is crisp and golden. Alternatively, make the meat sauce into a chili by adding a teaspoon of chili powder with the garlic, and a can of drained and rinsed kidney beans with the chopped tomatoes.

"One of the best ways to fight poverty and fight terrorism is to educate girls and bring women into the formal labor force."

Sheryl WuDunn

Spinach and fennel risotto

8oz spinach, washed

1 tablespoon olive oil

3 tablespoons butter

1 onion, finely chopped

1 fennel bulb, thinly sliced

½ cup dry white wine

1¾ cups risotto rice

4 cups chicken or vegetable stock

¼ cup walnuts, toasted and finely chopped

shavings of Parmesan cheese, to serve

salt and freshly ground black pepper

This risotto is both comforting and sophisticated. Quick enough for a satisfying weeknight supper.

Prepare 10 minutes | **Cook** 30 minutes | **Serves** 4

1 Steam the spinach over a pan of simmering water for 2 minutes until wilted. Drain well then chop finely. Heat the oil with half the butter in a large pan over medium heat, and add the onion and fennel. Cook for 5–7 minutes or until softened but not browned. Add the wine and simmer for a few minutes until the fennel is tender. Add the rice and stir to coat the grains in the juices.

2 Meanwhile, pour the stock into a separate pan and heat until simmering. Gradually add the simmering stock to the rice, a ladleful at a time, allowing each addition to be absorbed before adding more, until the rice is almost tender and two-thirds of the stock has been added. This will take about 15 minutes. Stir in the spinach and continue adding the remaining stock, a little at a time, until the rice is tender.

3 Remove from the heat and stir in the remaining butter and the walnuts. Season to taste, then serve in warm bowls topped with shavings of Parmesan.

"Martin Luther King once said,
'Our lives begin to end the day we become silent about things that matter.'
I printed it and put it on my desk in the office to remind myself
I am very much alive every day!"

Livia Firth

Pasta with broccoli, chile, and garlic

2 broccoli crowns, cut into florets

½ cup extra virgin olive oil plus 4 tablespoons to serve

5–6 garlic cloves, thinly sliced

1 teaspoon red pepper flakes

1 lb dried orecchiette pasta

¹/₃ cup pine nuts, toasted

handful of fresh basil leaves

½ cup Parmesan cheese, grated or shaved

salt and freshly ground black pepper

I love this pasta recipe: it is incredibly easy, fresh and super healthy. It's perfect for vegetarians, and can easily be varied for non-veggies by replacing the pine nuts with anchovies or by playing with more fresh ingredients as you go along.

Prepare 5 minutes | **Cook** 10 minutes | **Serves** 4

1 Bring a large pan of salted water to a boil, add the broccoli, and simmer for 3–4 minutes or until tender.

2 Meanwhile, heat the olive oil in a separate pan and gently cook the garlic and chile for 2–3 minutes or until the garlic is golden brown. When the broccoli florets are tender, scoop them out of the water with a slotted spoon and add to the pan with the garlic and chile along with ½ cup of the broccoli cooking water, reserving the remaining water. Using the back of a fork, crush the broccoli with the garlic to form a coarse purée.

3 Return the pan containing the broccoli cooking water to the heat and bring to a boil. Add the pasta and cook according to the package instructions until al dente. Drain thoroughly and pour into a large serving bowl. Top with the broccoli purée and drizzle with the additional olive oil. Scatter with the toasted pine nuts and basil leaves. Toss until evenly distributed. Season with freshly ground black pepper and serve with Parmesan.

Turkey
Syria
Iran
Saudi Arabia

IRAQ

Average WFWI participant

Age: 31-40

Married: 56% / Widowed: 14% / Single: 30%

Children: 2 / No. in household: 7

Literate: 88% / No formal education: 12%

Leyla's Story

Leyla is nearly 60 years old and lives near Baghdad. Her day-to-day existence during the war has been difficult. Despite life's challenges, Leyla and her husband Malik remained strong and built as normal a life for themselves as they could. Then one day in 2008, when walking the streets of Baghdad, they were caught in gunfire and both were shot. Malik did not survive. Leyla recovered, but the bullet that injured her struck her in the face, leaving her disfigured. She found herself alone, without a support network and lacking the skills to help support herself. She was depressed and traumatized from all she had been through.

"I was encouraged to sign up with Women for Women International and was matched with a sponsor. In December 2009, with the financial support of my new sponsor, I started attending classes with a group of 20 women. However, it was hard for me to engage in the program and training since I was embarrassed about my face and too shy to speak to the other women. For the first month of classes, I did not speak or participate. But after that, something changed in me. I became less afraid and found that I wanted to be part of the group. I chose to train in candle making and it made me feel worthwhile to have a skill. I also liked to help the other women in my group to learn. I can see the reflection of my beauty in the candles I have learned to make."

The changes Leyla has been able to make in her life are not only internal. She has been traveling to a hospital in Baghdad, where she continues to receive treatment to fix the scars on her face as much as possible. Although she will always have scars, her new-found confidence helps her to conquer her fears.

IRAQ

Population: 31,129,225

Square km: 438,317

GDP per capita: $4,200

Unemployment: 15%

Life expectancy:
Female : 72 years / Male:69 years

Conflict dates: 2003-present

Estimated military deaths: 4800

Estimated civilian deaths: 105,000-
1.4 million (Iraq Body Count Project)

Internally displaced persons: 1,332,380

Recipes from Iraq

Iraq has one of the longest food histories of any nation, going back 10,000 years. The world's first cookbooks were tablets found in ancient Iraqi ruins. The cuisine reflects the country's rich heritage and strong influences from Turkey and Iran. Iraq produces more than 80 percent of the world's date supply, but few other plants flourish because of the arid climate, meaning more than 70 percent of foodstuffs need to be imported. Two decades of economic turbulence have resulted in unpredictable supplies. When supplies are good, typical Iraqi meals begin with an appetizer (*mezze*), such as kebabs, then soup, a main course with meat and rice, salad and flatbread (*khubaz*), followed by rich, dark Iraqi coffee. The coffee's unique flavor is achieved by heating and cooling it nine times before it is served, to remove any impurities.

Qeema Q Timan

Still popular today, this traditional meat and chickpea recipe is often served at religious celebrations. Black lemons, or *loomi*, are actually dried limes. They are available from Middle Eastern stores or online spice suppliers.

Prepare 15 minutes | **Cook** 2½ hours | **Serves** 5-6

1¼ cups dried chickpeas
1 lb diced braising beef
2 tablespoons vegetable oil
2 medium onions, diced
2 medium tomatoes, chopped
2 tablespoons tomato paste
1 teaspoon Baharat spices
1 tablespoon crushed cardamom
2-3 dried black lemons, pricked
salt and freshly ground black pepper

1 Place the chickpeas in a large pan, cover with water, and bring to a boil. Reduce the heat to a simmer and cook for 1½–2 hours, or until they are soft. Drain the chickpeas and then mash them using a potato masher.
2 Meanwhile, place the beef in a separate pan and cover with about 6 cups of water. Place over medium heat, bring to a simmer, and cook for about 2 hours, or until the beef is tender.
3 When the meat is nearly tender, heat the oil in a pan over medium heat, and fry the onions, stirring, for 5 minutes or until the onions have browned. Add the tomatoes and cook for 5 more minutes, then mix in the tomato paste.
4 Add the meat with the liquid to the tomato mixture. Stir in the mashed chickpeas, Baharat spices, cardamom, and dried black lemon. Season and leave to simmer gently for 20 minutes. Serve with rice.

Timan Bagalah

This recipe of rice and beans is one of the most popular dishes in Iraq. It is common because it is easy and cheap to make, and is suitable for vegetarians. This dish is particularly famous in the central and southern areas of Iraq, especially the provinces of Basra and Nasiriyah.

Prepare 15 minutes, plus 30 minutes soaking | **Cook** 20-25 minutes | **Serves** 4

1¼ cups basmati rice
1 tablespoon vegetable oil
1 medium onion, chopped
$^2/_3$ cup fresh or frozen fava beans or edamame, shelled
6 tablespoons fresh dill, finely chopped

1 Soak the rice in water for about 30 minutes.
2 Meanwhile, heat the oil in a pan over medium heat, fry the onions gently for 3-4 minutes, or until softened. Stir in the beans and dill and cook for 2-3 minutes.
3 Drain the rice, put into a separate pan and pour in 1 cup water. Add some salt. Bring to a boil and simmer for 5 minutes, then drain. Add the rice to the pan with the bean mixture, stir and cook for 5 minutes or until the rice is cooked. Serve with yogurt and cucumber salad.

"Having lost a son to meningitis, I realise how important it is that every child is shown love. After such a tragic loss, I decided to use my skills to help others less fortunate than myself."

Alex Cooke

Pot-roasted silverside with shallots

2 tablespoons vegetable oil

2 lbs beef, rump roast or bottom round

20–25 shallots, peeled

3 garlic cloves, peeled and sliced

3 sprigs thyme

1 sprig rosemary

2 bay leaves

1¼ cups red wine

1 cup hot beef stock

3 tablespoons tomato paste

1 tablespoon cornstarch

salt and freshly ground black pepper

Prepare 10 minutes | **Cook** 3½ hours, plus resting time | **Serves** 8

1 Preheat the oven to 325°F. Heat the oil in a large Dutch oven with a well-fitting lid. Add the beef and sear over high heat for 4–5 minutes, turning regularly so that the outside of the beef is golden brown all over. Transfer to a plate and keep warm.

2 Add the shallots and garlic to the Dutch oven and cook for 2–3 minutes, or until starting to color. Meanwhile, make a bouquet garni by tying together the thyme, rosemary, and bay leaves with a piece of kitchen string. Add the red wine, beef stock, and tomato paste to the Dutch oven and stir. Return the beef to the pan, add the bouquet garni, season, and bring to a boil.

3 Cover and transfer to the oven for 3–3½ hours, turning the beef halfway through cooking. Then remove the beef, cover with foil, and keep warm. Allow to rest for 20 minutes before slicing. Remove the bouquet garni and discard.

4 To make the gravy thicker, add a little cold water to the cornstarch to form a paste, and stir it into the cooking liquid. Return the Dutch oven to the stove and bring to a boil, stirring until thickened. Thickly slice the beef, spoon the gravy over the top, and serve with plenty of creamy mashed potatoes and steamed greens.

"It matters how we use natural resources and that we understand our planet is finite. We can find better ways to fill our needs that protect the world around us."

Wendy Schmidt

Braised broccoli with garlic and lemon

3 tablespoons lemon-infused olive oil

2 broccoli crowns, cut into evenly sized florets

5–6 garlic cloves, sliced

zest of 1 lemon

salt and freshly ground black pepper

I adapted this recipe from a pasta dish that included braised sliced artichoke hearts. It is something I eat several times a week. Easy to make, healthy, fresh, and delicious. I'm in love with lemon olive oil.

Prepare 5 minutes | **Cook** 15 minutes | **Serves** 4

1 Heat the olive oil in a large, lidded, nonstick frying pan over medium-high heat. Add the broccoli with the garlic and a pinch of salt. Cook for 1–2 minutes or until beginning to soften, turning to coat lightly with the oil.

2 Add ½ cup water to the pan and reduce the heat to medium-low. Cover and cook for 4–5 minutes, or until the broccoli is just tender.

3 Add the lemon zest and raise the heat to high. Cook, stirring constantly to keep the broccoli moving, for 2–3 minutes or until the lemon zest softens and the garlic and broccoli just begin to caramelize. Season to taste and serve.

"What motivates me is a strong sense of social justice, as well as the mission to find the truth through first-hand reporting. If we raise awareness of atrocities and speak truth to power there is more chance that legitimate grievances will be addressed."

Christiane Amanpour

Lemon, garlic, and rosemary roast chicken with hasselback roast potatoes

3–4 tablespoons butter, softened

½ cup fresh rosemary, finely chopped

4 lb whole chicken

1 tablespoon olive oil

2 lemons, halved

1 head of garlic, halved

salt and freshly ground black pepper

For the potatoes

1½ lbs Yukon gold potatoes, scrubbed

3 tablespoons olive oil

1 tablespoon chopped fresh rosemary

3 garlic cloves

I buy organic chicken with the giblets removed, season it with lemon, garlic, and rosemary, then pop it in the oven for a couple of hours, and out it comes! Delicious with roast or mashed potatoes, green beans and broccoli, or salad. My family loves it!

Prepare 20 minutes | **Cook** 2 hours | **Serves** 4

1 Preheat the oven to 350°F. Place the butter and rosemary in a small bowl, season, and mix well.

2 Ease your hand under the skin of the chicken at the neck opening and smear the herb butter under the skin. Rub all over with the oil and squeeze the juice of 1 of the lemons over the chicken, then place the remaining lemon and squeezed lemon shells inside the chicken along with garlic. Season and place on a roasting pan.

3 Calculate the cooking time, allowing 20 minutes per pound plus 15 minutes. Roast until the juices run clear and there is no pink meat. Remove from the oven and baste. Rest for 10 minutes before carving.

4 About an hour before the chicken is finished, prepare the potatoes. Cut thin vertical slits two thirds of the way down each one so that the bases of the potatoes stay whole (and so they resemble little toast racks).

5 Toss the potatoes in the olive oil with the rosemary and garlic cloves and season, making sure the oil goes right down into the slits. Scatter the potatoes around the outside of the chicken in the roasting pan and cook for 45–50 minutes, until golden brown and crisp, turning occasionally.

6 Carve the chicken and serve with the potatoes.

"I don't think people understand that being poor means you have to work from dawn until dusk just to survive through the day... I want a different world. One where I don't wake up thinking I'm so lucky to be able to feed my daughter."

Emma Thompson

Sausage and cabbage casserole

12 sausages
1–2 large Savoy cabbages
1 stick butter
salt and freshly ground
black pepper

This is one of my favorite winter recipes and is ridiculously easy. You need really good sausages, though. I use Toulouse from a deli, but all the supermarkets sell good sausages these days, so you don't have to be all fancy about it.

Prepare 10 minutes | **Cook** 3 hours | **Serves** 4–6

1 Preheat the oven to 300°F. Remove the sausage meat from the skins and set aside. Remove the leaves from the cabbages, discarding the outer leaves and the stalk. Blanch the leaves in boiling water for 3–4 minutes then plunge into cold water. Drain and dry thoroughly with paper towels.

2 Arrange a layer of cabbage leaves in the bottom of a large ovenproof casserole with a tight-fitting lid. Dot with butter, and follow with a layer of sausage meat and seasoning. Repeat to form 3–4 tightly packed layers, ending with the thicker cabbage leaves on top, which will act as a lid.

3 Cover and cook in the oven for 3 hours or until it's all soft and gooey. Serve with baked potatoes.

"The key to improving an impoverished community is by working at the grassroots. Helping families to rise up from abject poverty enables them to reach out and support others in their community."

Tom Steuart-Feilding

Sweet potato-topped salmon and spinach pie

1 cup milk
3/4 cup fish stock
1 lb salmon fillet
8oz cooked shrimp
8oz spinach
5 tablespoons butter
2/3 cup all-purpose flour
2 tablespoons fresh dill, chopped
3/4 cup sour cream
1½ lbs large white potatoes, peeled and cut into even-sized pieces
1½ lbs sweet potatoes, peeled and cut into even-sized pieces
salt and freshly ground black pepper

A colorful take on a traditional fish pie, topped with mashed sweet potato for a more complex flavor.

Prepare 30 minutes | **Cook** 1 hour | **Serves** 4–6

1 Preheat the oven to 400°F. Pour the milk and stock into a large roasting pan and add the salmon. Cook in the oven for 12–15 minutes or until the fish is just opaque and cooked through. Transfer the fish to a plate, reserving the cooking liquid. Break the fish into large chunks, discarding the skin, then arrange the fish with the shrimp in a shallow 2-quart baking dish.

2 Wash the spinach and place in a pan with the water still clinging to the leaves. Place on low heat for 2–3 minutes or until wilted, then drain thoroughly. Add to the dish containing the salmon and shrimp.

3 Melt 3 tablespoons of the butter in a medium pan over low heat, add the flour, and cook, stirring, for 1 minute. Remove from the heat and gradually add the reserved fish cooking liquid, stirring well after each addition, to form a smooth sauce. Return to the heat and bring to a boil, stirring constantly, then simmer for 3–5 minutes, stirring occasionally. Remove from the heat and stir in the dill and sour cream. Season, pour over the fish and spinach, and set aside to cool.

4 Cook the potatoes and sweet potatoes separately in two large pans of boiling water for 15 minutes or until tender. Drain and mash, then mix the remaining butter into the plain potato, and season. Stir the two mashes together but don't overmix. Spoon the mashed potatoes over the fish and spinach to cover completely. Cook for 35–40 minutes until golden brown and crisp on top. Serve with green vegetables.

"Happy, healthy children are our future, our pride and joy."
WfWI Rwanda participant

"I work to limit climate change because it's the biggest problem human beings have ever faced—or really, so far, not faced. Many of the people who will suffer most have done the least to cause the problem, so it's both a practical and a moral crisis."

Bill McKibben

Bill McKibben: Tandoori yogurt chicken

1 whole chicken, approx. 3 lbs, cut
into 8 pieces and skin removed

1 teaspoon salt

juice of 1 lemon

For the yogurt marinade

2 cups Greek yogurt

1 onion, coarsely chopped

3 garlic cloves, crushed

1-inch piece fresh ginger
peeled and grated

1–2 red chiles, seeded and
chopped

¼ teaspoon ground turmeric

2 teaspoons garam masala

red food coloring (optional)

To serve

handful of cilantro leaves

lime or lemon wedges

I love India. The noise, the color, the goodness of the people, and the food all attract me. I love the vegetarian food of the south, especially Kerala, but I've never really learned to duplicate my favorite of all (the dosa) at home. Madhur Jaffrey, whose recipe I've adapted here, was instrumental in introducing Americans to good Indian food, and I've always been grateful.

Prepare 25 minutes, plus 8 hours marinating | **Cook** 25 minutes | **Serves** 4

1 Using a sharp knife, cut deep slashes into the thickest parts of the chicken, but do not cut as far as the bone. Place the chicken pieces into a large bowl and sprinkle with the salt and lemon juice. Rub well all over the chicken. Set aside for 20 minutes.

2 Meanwhile, make the marinade. Place the yogurt, onion, garlic, ginger, chiles, turmeric, and garam masala into a blender or food processor, and blend until smooth. Add the red food coloring, if using.

3 Rub the marinade into the chicken, rubbing it well into the slits in the meat. Cover and refrigerate for at least 8 hours, and up to 24 hours.

4 Preheat the broiler to high or light a barbecue. Cook the chicken for about 20–25 minutes, turning regularly, or until it is thoroughly cooked, there is no pink flesh, and the juices run clear. Scatter with fresh cilantro leaves, and serve with wedges of lemon or lime.

Cook's tip

Alternatively, use 8 large chicken pieces such as thighs, drumsticks, and breasts.

"It's not even a question. We all have a social responsibility and all of us can, in some way, be a beacon of light."

Alek Wek

Okra stew

2 tablespoons vegetable oil
2 medium onions, sliced
2 medium tomatoes, diced
1 fresh red or green chile, chopped (optional)
1 lb okra, cut into 1-inch lengths
3 cups chicken or vegetable stock
5 garlic cloves, finely chopped
salt and freshly ground black pepper

Okra is perfect for a stew because it helps to thicken the sauce. The heat of the chile gives this stew extra depth, great for a cold day, but it's also delicious without if you prefer.

Prepare 10 minutes | **Cook** 45 minutes | **Serves** 4

1 Heat the oil in a pan over medium heat, add the onions, and cook for about 5 minutes, or until they are starting to color. Stir in the tomatoes and simmer for 5 minutes. Season and add the chile, if using.

2 Stir in the okra and cook for 1–2 minutes. Pour in the stock and simmer for 15–20 minutes, or until the mixture has thickened, adding a little more water if needed. Add the garlic, reduce the heat, and continue to simmer for another 5–10 minutes. Serve with a bowl of steamed rice or pita bread.

Cook's tip
For a meaty version, reduce the amount of okra in the stew and replace it with cooked diced lamb or chicken breast. Add with the okra in Step 2.

"As a global citizen I believe that where and to whom and what gender you are born should not determine your destiny. The building blocks of opportunities such as education, health care and employment can transform lives."

Afshan Khan

Baghare baingan (eggplant curry)

2 large eggplants, about 1¹⁄₃ lbs
8 tablespoons vegetable oil
2 large onions, sliced
¼ teaspoon ground turmeric
1 garlic clove, crushed to a paste
1-inch piece fresh ginger, peeled and grated
1 teaspoon chili powder
1½ teaspoons ground cumin
½ teaspoon garam masala
4 tablespoons coconut cream, or
½ cup coconut milk
juice of ½ lemon
rice or hot chapati, to serve

Prepare 10 minutes | **Cook** 25 minutes | **Serves** 4 as a side dish

1 Cut the eggplants in half lengthwise, then cut each half into quarters. Heat 2 tablespoons of the oil in a large frying pan over medium heat and cook the eggplant in batches for 4–5 minutes, or until golden brown, adding more oil as necessary. Set aside on a plate lined with paper towels.

2 Return the pan to the heat and add 3 tablespoons of the oil. Add the onions and cook for 8–10 minutes, or until softened and brown. Add the turmeric, garlic, ginger, chili powder, cumin, and garam masala and cook, stirring, for 1–2 minutes.

3 Add the coconut cream or coconut milk with ²⁄₃ cup of water to make a sauce. Add the lemon juice and return the eggplant to the pan. Cook on low-medium heat for 5–6 minutes or until the oil floats on top or can be seen on the sides of the pan. Serve accompanied by rice or hot chapatis.

Cook's tip

If garam masala is not available, combine 1 teaspoon of cinnamon and coriander with 2 pinches of nutmeg and 2 ground cloves.

"We believe in people helping people, and we're on a mission to transform people's lives and support the environment by encouraging a more natural, organic and holistic way of living."

Peter Kindersley

Spinach and tomato dahl

2 tablespoons olive oil

2 red onions, finely chopped

4 garlic cloves, minced

2-inch piece of fresh ginger, peeled and grated

1 green chile, finely sliced

1 teaspoon cumin seeds

½ teaspoon ground coriander

½ teaspoon ground turmeric

pinch of asafetida (optional)

½ teaspoon salt

1 cup red lentils

14-oz can chopped tomatoes

4 cups vegetable stock or water

8oz baby spinach, washed

To serve

steamed basmati rice

warm naan or pita bread

4 generous tablespoons thick, creamy, plain yogurt

handful of fresh cilantro, parsley or mint, or a combination of the three

1 lemon or lime, cut into wedges

Health is at the heart of everything we do at Neal's Yard, and we believe that by supporting an organic lifestyle we are acting as responsible stewards for our environment, ensuring a future for the next generation. I've chosen this recipe because it's organic, quick and easy, and more importantly it's healthy, hearty, and perfect for the whole family. An easy but elegant dahl, it provides a real burst of color on the plate as the brilliant green of the spinach sets off the sunset orange lentils.

Prepare 15 minutes | **Cook** 45 minutes | **Serves** 4

1 Heat the oil in a lidded, wide, heavy-bottomed pan over medium heat. Add the onion, garlic, ginger, and chile, and cook, stirring often, for about 10 minutes or until the onions have softened. Add the cumin, coriander, turmeric, asafetida (if using), and salt. Stir and cook for 2 minutes, or until fragrant.

2 Stir in the lentils, tomatoes, and stock or water and bring to a boil. Cover, reduce the heat to a slow simmer, and cook for about 20–30 minutes, or until the lentils are soft and thick, stirring often to prevent them from sticking to the bottom of the pan.

3 Fold in the spinach and cook for 3–5 minutes, or until it has wilted. Adjust the seasoning, then serve with steamed basmati rice and warm naan or pita bread. Top each serving with a generous spoonful of yogurt, scatter lavishly with the chopped fresh herbs, and pass around the citrus wedges for everyone to squeeze over their dishes.

Cook's tip

You can cook the lentils several days ahead and refrigerate until needed, but stir in the spinach just before serving so it retains its color.

"A son was born to us in 1976 who failed to develop and was later diagnosed as profoundly disabled. This sweet child has grown into a gentle, peaceful young man who does not speak, dress himself, or have the ability to meet his own basic needs. He has been a source of love and insight. Through him we came to see a segment of society that we had been previously blind to—the poor and needy."

Don and Deyon Stephens

Thai green chicken curry

14oz can coconut milk
2 tablespoons green Thai curry paste
1 large red bell pepper, seeded and thinly sliced
1 onion, thinly sliced
1 lb chicken breast, cut into 1-inch chunks
1 tablespoon brown sugar
1 tablespoon nam pla (fish sauce)
2 medium tomatoes, chopped
handful of fresh basil, thinly sliced
juice of 1 lime
steamed rice and fresh cilantro leaves, to serve
salt and freshly ground black pepper

This recipe is a favorite! It's so easy to make, we usually double or even triple the quantities to have later in the week and for lunch. Remember to simmer the curry paste in a little bit of the coconut milk before adding the rest in order to release its fragrance. It's especially tasty served over jasmine rice.

Prepare 10 minutes | **Cook** 20 minutes | **Serves** 4

1 Pour 1/2 cup of the coconut milk into a large frying pan over medium-high heat. Stir in the curry paste and bring to a boil, stirring continuously.

2 Add the bell pepper and onion and cook for 5 minutes, or until softened. Stir in the chicken with the remaining coconut milk, and add the sugar and nam pla. Simmer for about 10 minutes or until the chicken is thoroughly cooked through and there is no pink meat.

3 Add the tomatoes, basil leaves, and lime juice and simmer for 2–3 minutes, or until piping hot. Season, scatter with the cilantro leaves, and serve with steamed rice.

"I wholeheartedly support the work WfWI does to empower women to rebuild their lives and their communities, to claim their rights as human beings, and plant hope in their hearts for a better life for themselves and their families."

Cherie Lunghi

Roast pork fillet with five-spice plum sauce

1 pork tenderloin, about 1 lb, trimmed

2 tablespoons olive oil

1 tablespoon sesame seeds

salt and freshly ground black pepper

For the plum sauce

1 shallot or ½ small onion, finely chopped

1 garlic clove, minced

1 lb plums, pitted and roughly chopped

2 tablespoons brown sugar

2 tablespoons soy sauce

1 tablespoon Chinese five-spice powder

Prepare 10 minutes | **Cook** 40 minutes | **Serves** 4

1 Preheat the oven to 400°F. Rub the pork with a tablespoon of the oil and roll it in the sesame seeds. Season and roast in the oven for 15–20 minutes, or until the juices run clear.

2 Meanwhile, make the plum sauce. Heat the remaining oil in a pan over medium heat, add the shallot or onion and garlic, and cook gently for 2–3 minutes, or until softened. Stir in the plums and sugar, cover, and simmer gently for 5 minutes or until the plums have softened and the mixture has thickened. Stir in the soy sauce and five-spice powder, and cook for 2–3 minutes.

3 Remove the pork from the oven, place on a warm serving plate, and leave to rest for 10 minutes before slicing thickly and serving with the plum sauce and stir-fried vegetables such as bok choi or broccoli, or Alice Walker's Steamed greens with oyster sauce (below).

"Is solace anywhere more comforting than in the arms of a sister?"

Alice Walker

Steamed greens with oyster sauce

3 tablespoons olive oil

2 garlic cloves, chopped

1 cup scallions, sliced

1 lb mixed greens, such as kale and spinach

soy sauce, to taste

oyster sauce, to taste

½ teaspoon cayenne pepper or red pepper flakes (optional)

Greens, especially collards, are so easy to grow. A mainstay of African Americans on the plantations during the long period of enslavement, they remained beloved ever after. It is believed that our symbiotic relationship with greens accounts for the beautiful skin of our people and for our dense, strong and resilient bones.

Prepare 5 minutes | **Cook** 20 minutes | **Serves** 4

1 Heat the olive oil in a large heavy-bottomed pan over medium heat. Add the garlic and scallions and cook gently for 5–10 minutes, or until softened. Remove from the heat and set aside.

2 Wash and roughly chop the greens, then return the pan to high heat. Add the kale (you should hear a sizzle as the greens hit the pan) and cook for 3 minutes then add the spinach and cook for 3–5 minutes more, or until wilted, stirring with a wooden spoon. Add splashes of soy sauce and oyster sauce, to taste, as well as the cayenne pepper or red pepper flakes (if using).

3 Serve with baked potatoes, rice, cornbread, scrambled eggs, chicken, fish or pork.

DEMOCRATIC REPUBLIC OF CONGO

Average WfWI participant

Age: 18-24

Married: 75% / Widowed: 12% / Single: 13%

Children: 4 / No. in household: 7

Literate: 31% / No formal education: 38%

Christine's story

Rape is a shameful act wherever it occurs. Sadly, in the Democratic Republic of Congo that shame is conferred upon the blameless woman, who is shunned by her husband, family and society. To speak publicly of such a terrible trauma is hard enough in the Western world - if you do so in the DRC, you are likely to be judged and rejected.

"I was just 14 when I lost my parents. Before I was 20, I married and had three children. When I turned 24, war broke out near my home in Masisi. There was so much violence. The militia took us all to the bush and killed my husband. I managed to escape along with my children and reached Mugunga Refugee Camp.

Life in the camp was so difficult. There was little economic support and so much violence. One day when I was collecting firewood in the bush in order to cook for my children, I was raped and became pregnant.

While pregnant I was taken care of by the UN Refugee Agency (UNHCR). That was when I heard about Women for Women International. I heard there was a group that defended the rights of women. I was given a place in the classes. When I first went, I felt that I was not like other women. I am an orphan, then a widow, then a rape victim. I was so depressed I could not speak.

Women for Women International taught me how to manage the stress in my life, and I learned how to bake. Now I am in a food cooperative with 20 women and I am the vice president. We bake and sell our goods for profit. Women for Women International provided me with the training and the tools to earn money so I can survive. The group helped me to understand I am a woman just like other women."

As Christine speaks, the sorrow and shame cloud her face. Her head hangs low and her voice becomes very soft and tremulous. Meanwhile, the beautiful little girl in her arms, the product of that terrible act, sleeps peacefully.

DEMOCRATIC REPUBLIC OF CONGO (DRC)

Population: 73,599,190

Square km: 2,344,858

GDP per capita: $300

Life expectancy:
Female : 57 years / Male:54 years

Conflict dates: 1998-2003; ongoing in
eastern Congo

Total no. killed: 5.4 million (estimated)

Internally displaced persons: 1,709,280

Recipes from the Democratic Republic of Congo

The Congolese used to be able to count on one substantial meal a day, but this is no longer the case. The lack of food is largely blamed on government neglect, as less than 1 percent of the national budget goes to agriculture. It is not surprising, therefore, that less than 2 percent of the land in the DRC is cultivated, and what is is mostly subsistence farming. Typical crops are corn, rice, cassava (manioc), sweet potatoes, plantains, tomatoes, pumpkin, peas, and some nuts. Congolese food varies widely, representing the huge diversity of the indigenous people in the country. The primary staple is *fufu*, made from cassava tubers pounded into the texture of oatmeal and eaten from a communal bowl. Depending on wealth, season, and availability, it is accompanied by side dishes of sweet potatoes, bananas, plantains, and sometimes fish such as perch. Meat is a delicacy for special days or for those who can afford such a luxury. For people lucky enough to live near a river or stream, fish is a primary food source, and families often build their own ponds by diverting small rivers using bamboo for pipes. After six months of feeding, the fish are harvested and then either salted or smoked to sell at markets during the year.

Corn fritters with pineapple salsa

Prepare 15 minutes | **Cook** 20 minutes | **Makes** 16-20

1 cup all-purpose flour
2 teaspoons baking powder
a pinch of paprika
2 eggs
1 cup milk
1¼ cups canned corn kernels
¼ cup scallions or shallots, sliced
¼ cup chopped parsley, cilantro, basil, or baby spinach
1-2 hot red chiles, minced
vegetable oil, for frying
salt and freshly ground black pepper

For the pineapple salsa
½ cup fresh pineapple, finely chopped
1 large red chile, seeded and finely chopped
1 teaspoon brown sugar
1 teaspoon soy sauce
1 tablespoon cilantro
juice of 1 lime, to taste

1 Place the flour in a large bowl with the baking powder and a pinch of paprika and season with salt and pepper. Stir to combine.
2 Beat together the eggs and milk, then gradually add to the dry ingredients to form a smooth batter. Stir in the corn, scallions or shallots, chopped herbs, and chiles.
3 In a frying pan heat a little vegetable oil, then drop heaping spoonfuls of batter into the pan in batches. Cook for 2-3 minutes per side.
4 Combine the ingredients for the salsa and serve with the cooked corn fritters, a spinach salad, and a spoonful of sour cream.

Doughnuts

Prepare 30 minutes plus 2 hours rising | **Cook** 35 minutes | **Makes** 16

1 cup milk
4 cups all-purpose flour, plus extra for dusting
1 teaspoon active dry yeast
2 tablespoon sugar
1 teaspoon salt
4 cups vegetable oil
2 large eggs, beaten
1 cup sugar

1 Gently warm the milk in a heavy saucepan, remove from the heat and set aside.
2 Put 3 cups of the flour in the bowl of an electric mixer with a dough hook, and mix in the yeast, sugar, and salt. Then pour the warm milk into the flour with 2 tablespoons of the oil and and the eggs. Gradually mix in the remaining flour until you have a soft dough, then knead for 3-4 minutes (or 6-8 minutes if mixing by hand), until smooth and elastic. Transfer to a clean bowl, then cover and let the dough rise in a warm place until doubled in size about 1½ hours.
3 Divide into 16 equal-sized portions and roll into balls. Transfer to a floured towel, cover with a piece of oiled plastic wrap, and let rise in a warm place for 30 minutes.
4 Heat the remaining oil in a large, heavy saucepan to 375° F. Fry the doughnuts one by one for about 2 minutes each, until golden. Drain onto a plate lined with paper towels. Pour the sugar onto a plate and roll the warm cooked doughnuts in the sugar before serving.

*"I believe that we should all help each other,
but especially those who are less fortunate."*

Dame Judi Dench

Bread and butter pudding

1 lb panettone
4 tablespoons butter, softened,
plus extra for greasing
2 tablespoons candied lemon or
orange peel, finely chopped
2 tablespoons currants or raisins
1½ cups milk
¾ cup heavy cream
zest of ½ lemon
¼ cup sugar
3 eggs, beaten
grated nutmeg, to taste

This is delicious and provides the perfect solution for what to do with those Italian cakes you are given at Christmas!

Prepare 10 minutes | **Cook** 40 minutes | **Serves** 6–12, depending on portion size!

1 Preheat the oven to 350°F. Grease a 1-quart rectangular baking dish.
2 Slice the panettone into ½ –1 inch slices and butter each slice. Cut the buttered slices into quarters and arrange over the base of the prepared baking dish to cover. Sprinkle with the candied peel and half the currants or raisins. Arrange another layer of panettone in the dish and sprinkle with the remaining currants or raisins.
3 Combine the milk and cream with the lemon zest and sugar, then add the beaten eggs, and stir to combine.
4 Pour the milk, cream, and egg mixture over the panettone and sprinkle with freshly grated nutmeg. Bake in the oven for 30–40 minutes until just set and browned on top, and serve warm. This is delicious with Butterscotch sauce (below).

Butterscotch sauce

¹/₃ cup brown sugar
²/₃ cup heavy cream
4 tablespoons butter

Prepare 2 minutes | **Cook** 10 minutes | **Makes** 250ml

1 Place the sugar in a pan over medium heat and add 1 tablespoon water. Heat, stirring, until the sugar has dissolved, then bring to a boil and cook for 5–7 minutes, or until you have a dark caramel. Whisk in the cream, then the butter. Serve drizzled over the the Bread and butter pudding (above) with a scoop of ice cream or whipped cream.

"When I am walking the roads in my country and I am all by myself, I know there is a woman out there who cares for me, and I am thankful to have a sponsor."

Honorata, WfWI Democratic Republic of Congo participant

Kate Spade: Gooey chocolate brownies

2 sticks unsalted butter
12oz unsweetened chocolate (70% cocoa solids), broken into squares
4 large eggs
1½ cups brown sugar
1 teaspoon vanilla extract
1¾ cups all-purpose flour, sifted
1¾ cups walnut or pecan nuts, roughly chopped

These brownies are the perfect treat: rich and chocolatey, and satisfyingly gooey in the middle.

Prepare 20 minutes | **Cook** 25 minutes | **Makes** 16

1 Preheat the oven to 350°F. Grease and line a 9 x 12 inch baking pan.

2 Melt the butter and chocolate together in a small saucepan over low heat, stirring regularly. When the lumps of chocolate are fairly small, turn off the heat—there will be enough residual heat to melt the chocolate completely and you reduce the risk of overheating the mixture. Allow to cool.

3 Place the eggs, sugar, and vanilla into a large bowl and whisk for 10 minutes, or until pale and fluffy. Stir the chocolate mixture into the egg mixture, then fold in the flour and chopped nuts.

4 Pour the mixture into the prepared pan and bake in the oven for 20–25 minutes or until a cake tester or toothpick inserted near the edge comes out clean. The mixture should still be a little gooey in the middle. Allow to cool in the pan, then cut into 16 squares and serve.

"When we make our food choices, it's important to remember the hungry, the exploited and those who don't have any real food options. Children around the world are suffering from malnutrition, despite there being enough food for everyone."

Ellen Gustafson

Apple and berry oat crumble

softened butter, for greasing

2 apples of different varieties, peeled and cored

1¼ cups fresh or frozen berries (blueberries, cherries, raspberries, blackberries, or any combination)

¼ cup dried cranberries or cherries

brown sugar, to taste

For the crumble topping

⅓ cup oats

⅓ cup whole-wheat, spelt, or other wholegrain flour

1 tablespoon mixed seeds and chopped nuts, such as sunflower seeds, flaked almonds, chopped pecans or walnuts

1 teaspoon brown sugar

1 teaspoon ground cinnamon

5 tablespoons butter, melted

I love any recipe that can be adjusted depending on what you happen to have in the kitchen. I always have apples, frozen berries, oats, and cinnamon on hand and love that I can make a quick and healthy dessert for any last-minute visitors. The apples and cinnamon make the dessert taste warm and cozy, but can easily be left out if you prefer an all-berry crumble.

Prepare 10 minutes | **Cook** 40 minutes | **Serves** 2–4

1 Preheat the oven to 350°F. Generously grease a 1-quart ovenproof dish or large ramekin. Thinly slice the apples and combine with the berries and dried cranberries or cherries in the prepared baking dish. Sweeten to taste with a little sugar.

2 To make the crumble topping, place the oats, flour, seeds and nuts, sugar, and cinnamon in a bowl and stir in the melted butter. The mixture should be moist but crumbly. Spoon the topping evenly over the fruit.

3 Bake for 35–40 minutes, or until the crumble is golden brown and the apples are cooked and tender. Serve warm with cream, ice cream, or yogurt.

Cook's tip

Give this recipe a summery feel by replacing the apples with extra berries, or nectarines or peaches, and serving the crumble with a scoop of vanilla ice cream.

"Saudi women who succeed and excel regardless of all the obstacles they face every day are my biggest inspiration. Once upon a time, women in the West had few rights, but they fought for equality. I salute them. I hope my future daughters and granddaughters will enjoy their rights and even take them for granted."

Manal Alsharif

Basbosa

8 tablespoons butter, melted and cooled

2 eggs

1 cup sugar

3 tablespoons milk

1 cup heavy cream

1 teaspoon baking powder

½ teaspoon vanilla extract

1¾ cups cornstarch

½ cup dried coconut

²/₃ cup almonds or pistachio nuts, chopped

For the syrup

1 cup sugar

½ tablespoon lemon juice

My best time when I was a kid was when we had guests. My mother would make Basbosa, a traditional dessert originating from Egypt, that our grandmothers enjoyed, and we and our children are still enjoying today. It's very easy and quick to make, and tastes like nothing else.

Prepare 10 minutes | **Cook** 30 minutes | **Serves** 6–8

1 Preheat the oven to 350°F. Grease a 8 x 10 inch high-sided cake pan.

2 Pour the cooled melted butter into a mixing bowl and add the eggs, sugar, milk, cream, baking powder, and vanilla extract. Beat well with a hand-held electric mixer until the mixture is smooth.

3 Fold in the cornstarch and coconut, and mix until evenly combined. Spoon the mixture into the prepared cake pan and bake in the oven for 25–30 minutes, or until golden. Allow to cool in the pan until lukewarm.

4 Meanwhile, make the syrup. Place the sugar and lemon juice in a pan with 1/2 cup water. Place over low-medium heat and stir until the sugar has dissolved. Bring to a simmer and cook for 3–5 minutes, or until it is of a good syrupy consistency. Set aside to cool.

5 Drizzle the syrup over the lukewarm Basbosa, sprinkle with the chopped almonds or pistachio nuts, and serve.

WOMEN *for* WOMEN
International

community

recipes for sharing,
inspired by WfWI farm produce

"According to the Food and Agriculture Organization of the United Nations, Women are 70 percent of the world's farmers, produce 90 percent of the world's staple food crops, and yet own less than 2 percent of land. Investing in women's agricultural efforts is key to achieving global food security."

Zainab Salbi, Founder of WfWI

WOMEN *for* WOMEN
International

"We women used to depend on our husbands to provide funds, but through this project we have become self-reliant, and at the same time, we contribute to the well-being of our families and strengthen our comunities."

WfWI South Sudan participant

Women have a critical role to play in battling hunger and in rebuilding communities shattered by war. Earning money and becoming self-sufficient are two critical issues for socially excluded women and their families. By getting involved in agriculture, women can both generate their own income and grow or raise their own food. In 2011, over half of all WfWI's participants (more in the Democratic Republic of Congo, Rwanda, Nigeria, and South Sudan) enrolled in either agriculture or livestock vocational skills training as part of WfWI's 12-month education program.

WfWI provides agriculture and livestock training via an agribusiness approach. It does not just train women in agriculture, but also in how to turn it into a viable business that can earn them an income. Every WfWI participant receives intensive classroom and hands-on field training in farming or raising livestock, along with basic business training. Moreover, WfWI helps participants gain access to market partners, financial institutions, and legal services for increased economic empowerment. The participants learn to cultivate a variety of crops, from berries and melons to spinach, okra, potatoes, sorghum, maize, cassava, amaranthus, and peanuts. They learn to raise livestock, including poultry for meat and eggs, goats and pigs for meat, cows for dairy products, and bees for honey and wax. The food they produce is reflected in the recipes in this chapter.

The farming facilities serve as a central meeting point for the women who work there, building communities and relationships that cross tribal and spatial boundaries. WfWI strongly encourages women to form group and cooperative businesses. Cooperative farming enables smallholder women farmers to increase their collective efficiency, sustainability, and overall economic security. Women who choose to work collaboratively receive additional guidance and training during the year-long program, and up to four months after graduation. WfWI program participants are encouraged to save throughout the year to purchase or rent land. Over time, with sustained guidance, these groups will work as independent, legally registered agribusiness cooperatives capable of providing income and economic stability for women. This positively impacts on the community as a whole, while inspiring other communities and countries to engage women as vital participants in sustainable solutions to the world's problems.

"Sometimes the problem seems so big that changing one life doesn't feel like enough. But it is."

America Ferrera

Chicken fajitas with corn salsa

1 teaspoon ground cumin

½ teaspoon red pepper flakes

¼ teaspoon cinnamon

1 lb skinless chicken breasts

1 tablespoon vegetable oil

2 red or orange peppers, deseeded and sliced

8 floury tortillas

salt and freshly ground black pepper

For the salsa

7oz can corn, drained

6 scallions, sliced

1 red chile, seeded and chopped

2 tablespoons fresh cilantro leaves

juice of 1 lime

2 teaspoons brown sugar

To serve

sour cream

guacamole

shredded lettuce leaves

This is a great sharing meal, since you can set out all the components and let everyone help themselves. The slight spice of the fajitas is complemented by the fresh sweetness of the salsa, which is given an extra kick with some chile.

Prepare 10 minutes | **Cook** 30 minutes | **Serves** 4

1 Preheat the oven to 400°F. In a small bowl, mix together the cumin, red pepper flakes, and cinnamon and season. Rub the spice mix all over the chicken breasts to coat. Place in a small roasting pan and drizzle with the oil, add the peppers, and roast in the oven for 25–30 minutes, or until the chicken is thoroughly cooked and there is no pink meat.

2 Meanwhile, make the salsa. In a small bowl, mix together the corn, scallions, chile, and cilantro, and season. Stir in the lime juice and sugar.

3 Warm the tortillas in a nonstick frying pan over medium heat for about a minute on each side. Slice the chicken and serve with the peppers, salsa, warm floury tortillas, sour cream, guacamole, and shredded lettuce.

"I'm honored to join WfWI in envisaging a world where everyone is free to define the scope of their life and their future and to strive to achieve their full potential."

Najat Kaanache

Magical banana Creole cake

1 cup sugar
½ cup extra virgin olive oil
6 bananas, cut lengthwise (overly ripened bananas are deliciously sweet)
2 ½ cups multigrain flour
1 tablespoon cornstarch
1 tablespoon baking powder
½ teaspoon baking soda
½ teaspoon salt
4 large eggs, separated
1 cup milk
2 tablespoons plain yogurt
1 cup brown sugar
½ cup maple syrup

My mother used to bake banana cake before sunrise so the magical aromas would fill the house and we would awake feeling warm, loved and hungry.

Prepare 20 minutes | **Cook** 40 minutes | **Serves** 8

1 Preheat the oven to 350°F. Evenly spread the sugar in a 9-inch round 3-inch deep cake pan and heat over medium heat until the sugar melts and takes on an amber color. Remove from the heat and mix in 2 tablespoons of the olive oil, making sure the caramel is spread evenly over the bottom of the pan.

2 Arrange half the bananas over the caramel base. Sift together the flour, cornstarch, baking powder, and baking soda into a bowl, add salt, and set aside. Whisk the egg yolks with the remaining oil and brown sugar until creamy and foamy. Stir in the yogurt and maple syrup. Gradually fold in the dry ingredients, alternating with the milk.

3 In a separate bowl, whisk the egg whites until soft peaks form and gently fold them into the batter. Pour half of the batter over the banana layer, then gently add another layer of bananas and top with the rest of the batter. Bake in the oven for about 40 minutes until a toothpick inserted into the middle comes out clean.

4 Remove the cake from oven and let stand for 10 minutes. Place a large platter or plate on top so you can quickly invert the cake pan and lift it off, exposing the gorgeous caramelized banana top.

RWANDA

Average WfWI participant

Age: 31-40

Married: 64% / Widowed: 11% / Single: 25%

Children: 2 / No. in household: 5

Literate: 66% / No formal education: 31%

Janviere's Story

At Women for Women International Rwanda, 70 percent of the participants lost a family member in the 1994 genocide, often both parents. At enrolment, the typical Rwandan trainee has been earning less than a dollar a day. By graduation they're typically making double that amount. Many go from a life of isolation to becoming members of a community for the first time since the genocide.

"I was 12 when the genocide started. I remember saying goodbye to my parents when I left on my 30-minute walk to school in Kigali, our capital. When I got back home that night, my house had been burned down and my parents and little brother brutally killed by the Hutu militia. A neighbor who was fleeing the area took me in his truck to my uncle and aunt's house in the countryside. I didn't know where else to go.

I lived with my aunt and uncle until I was 16. Then a local village man promised me a better life if I would marry him. I foolishly believed him. After we married, we moved to Kigali and had two children. When our son was two and our daughter just six months, my husband left one morning and never came back. I haven't heard from or seen him since. My relatives were too far away and too poor to help us. I had two small children to care for and no money.

A friend told me about Women for Women International. I needed the skills they were teaching women so that I could care for my children. When I got into their program, I felt hope for the first time since the genocide began. A lady named Janet was my sponsor and wrote to me. Her letters made me feel like there was someone who cared about me and was thinking about me. That helped me stay strong when I worried about how I was going to feed my children. I still think about her and thank God for her.

I took cooking classes as part of my training. I worked hard to learn every skill I was taught. Now I work in a restaurant in Kigali along with two other program graduates. Some of the women I work with are Hutus. We work together, forgiving and finding peace. We are friends. I have proved that I can provide for my children on my own. I can feed them and buy their school uniforms and be sure they go to school.

We are still rebuilding our lives in Rwanda. It's not always easy to forgive, but when we cook and eat together it helps us to heal. Sometimes we sing and dance together. My new community of friends lets me hope for a future that is based on trust."

RWANDA

Population: 11,689,696

Square km: 26,338

GDP per capita: $1,300

Life expectancy:
Female : 59 years / Male:57 years

Conflict dates: April–July 1994

Total no. killed: 800,000–1 million
(estimated)

Recipes from Rwanda

As Africa's smallest, most densely populated country, Rwanda has limited land suitable for crop cultivation and raising cattle, and agriculture largely consists of subsistence farming. Historically, the Hutus were the crop growers, eating a more vegetable-based diet, with typical staples being bananas, plantains, beans, sorghum (a type of grain), and cassava (a tuberous root), while the Tutsis were more likely to own cattle and so consumed more milk and dairy products, in particular a traditional drink of curdled milk. When possible, dishes made from small quantities of beef, goat, and chicken are enjoyed, but this is rare. More often, meals are *ugali*, a paste made from corn and water, *isombe*, made from mashed cassava leaves and served with dried fish, and *matoke*, a dish made from steamed or baked plantains. In rural areas, *urwagwa* (banana beer) is made from the fermented juice of bananas mixed with roasted sorghum flour. Beer features in traditional rituals and ceremonies but is usually only consumed by men.

Rwandan chicken casserole

A traditional chicken stew with celery and tomato sauce flavored with chiles.

Prepare 15 minutes | **Cook** 1 hour
| **Serves** 4

3 tablespoons vegetable oil
3–4 lb whole chicken, cut into pieces
1 onion, thinly sliced
3 large tomatoes, chopped
2 ribs celery, sliced
1 hot pimento or chile pepper, minced
1 cup chicken stock
salt and freshly ground black pepper, to taste

1 Heat the oil in a large pan, and cook the chicken pieces for 4–5 minutes per side until golden in color. Transfer the chicken pieces from the pan onto a plate. Return the pan to the heat and add the onion. Cook for 5 minutes, or until softened and golden brown. Return the chicken pieces to the pan with the tomatoes, celery, salt, and chile.
2 Pour in the stock, bring to a boil, and then reduce the heat and simmer for 30–40 minutes until the chicken is tender. Season to taste and serve with rice.

Beans with cassava

A classic Rwandan vegetarian accompaniment, which is made with mashed cassava.

Prepare 20 minutes | **Cook** 2 hours 10 minutes
| **Serves** 4

1 cup dried pinto, borlotti, or white beans
1½ cups cassava, cut into chunks
2 tablespoons vegetable oil
1 onion, sliced
4 ribs celery, chopped
salt and freshly ground black pepper

1 Soak the beans in plenty of water overnight. The following day, rinse the beans and place in a large pot half-full of water. Bring to a boil and simmer for about 2 hours, or until the beans are almost tender. Add the cassava and boil for about 10 minutes, or until it is almost cooked.
2 Meanwhile, heat the oil in a frying pan and cook the onion until almost tender. Stir in the celery and continue cooking for 5–10 minutes or until softened. Drain the beans and cassava, add them to the frying pan, and lightly mash the ingredients together. Season well and mix thoroughly. Serve with green vegetables or salad such as Kachumbari on page 147.

"I want a world in which no woman can be bought or sold and no man wants to buy or sell her. Even as a girl I longed for equality."
Ruchira Gupta

Khatte bharwan karele (stuffed bitter gourds)

1 lb bitter gourds
salt

For the stuffing
4 tablespoons mustard oil
2 cups onion, finely chopped
½ teaspoon ground turmeric
1 teaspoon kashmiri mirch powder or chili powder
2–3 green chiles, finely chopped
1-inch piece fresh ginger, peeled and finely chopped
flesh from 1 small mango

For the dry masala
½ teaspoon fennel seeds
2–3 fenugreek seeds
½ teaspoon onion seeds
½ teaspoon mustard seeds
½ teaspoon coriander seeds
½ teaspoon cumin seeds

To serve
handful of fresh cilantro
lemon wedges

This dish is made from a vegetable native to India. I love its bitter taste. The recipe is special to my father's family and was handed to me by my sister, who got it from my aunt. It reminds me of home-cooked meals with my aunts, sisters, and cousins cooking in the large kitchen, some making the paste, some chopping, and some marinating. Cooking was communal and festive.

Prepare 20 minutes, plus 1 hour salting | **Cook** 20 minutes | **Serves** 6, as a side

1 To prepare the bitter gourds, cut them in half lengthwise and scrape away the seeds to leave a hollow. Sprinkle salt all over the gourds to cover and set aside for at least an hour to allow the salt to absorb the bitter juices. Squeeze the gourds to remove as much juice as possible, then rinse and pat dry with paper towels.

2 Meanwhile, make the dry masala. Add all of the spices to a nonstick frying pan over medium heat and dry-fry for 1–2 minutes, or until lightly browned and releasing a spicy aroma. Tip into a small bowl and set aside to cool. Grind in a coffee or spice grinder, or using a mortar and pestle, to a coarse powder.

3 Next make the stuffing. Heat a little of the mustard oil in a pan over medium heat and add the onion. Cook for 4–5 minutes or until softened, then add the turmeric, kashmiri mirch powder or chili powder, chiles, ginger, and mango, and cook for another minute. Stuff into the hollows of the prepared gourds.

4 Return the pan to the heat and add the remaining mustard oil. Add the stuffed gourds and sprinkle with the dry masala. Season with salt to taste. Cook for 8–10 minutes, or until softened. Alternatively, place in a preheated oven (400°F) and bake for 20–25 minutes until tender.

5 Serve at room temperature, garnished with fresh cilantro and lemon wedges.

"People in poverty are citizens and customers with rights and economic power, not just people in need of a handout. They want to determine their own future. Our role is to help make this happen."

Gary White

Soda bread

Bread and water are basic, life-sustaining necessities. This simple recipe serves as a reminder that everyone deserves a safe drink of water and enough food to thrive.

Prepare 15 minutes | **Cook** 35 minutes | **Serves** 8

3 tablespoons butter, melted, plus extra for greasing
2 cups all-purpose flour, plus extra for dusting
1 2/3 cups whole-wheat flour
1½ teaspoons salt
1 teaspoon baking soda
1 cup plus 2 tablespoons buttermilk
5 tablespoons milk

1 Preheat the oven to 400°F. Grease a baking sheet. Mix the flours, salt and baking soda together in a bowl. Stir in the buttermilk, milk, and melted butter, and mix with a round-bladed knife to form a soft dough. Transfer to a floured surface and shape into a round. Transfer onto the prepared baking sheet and flatten slightly.

2 Dust generously with flour. Using a sharp knife, cut a deep cross into the top of the dough.

3 Bake in the oven for 35 minutes, or until risen and deep golden and the base of the bread sounds hollow when tapped. Transfer to a wire rack to cool before serving.

"The best way to reduce poverty is to empower women and help them become self-sufficient, so they can educate their children and create a different world for themselves. It's a huge goal, but it's really possible when everybody just does a little bit."

Marsha Wallace

Roasted tomato, mozzarella, and arugula pizza

8oz grape tomatoes, halved

3²/₃ cups bread flour, plus extra for dusting

1½ teaspoons salt

1 package or 1 teaspoon active dry yeast

2 tablespoons olive oil, plus extra for drizzling

6 tablespoons tomato or olive tapenade

1 small red onion, thinly sliced

5oz mozzarella cheese, torn into pieces

4oz wild arugula

²/₃ cup Parmesan cheese, shaved

Prepare 15 minutes, plus 1 hour rising | **Cook** 20 minutes | **Makes** 2

1 Preheat the oven to 325°F. Place the tomatoes on a baking sheet and cook in the oven for 20–30 minutes, or until softened and semi-dried but not browned.

2 Meanwhile, sift the flour and salt into a large bowl and stir in the yeast. Make a well in the center. Whisk half of the oil with 1¼ cups warm water and pour into the well. Mix into a soft dough and turn onto a floured surface. Knead for 10 minutes or until smooth and elastic. Put in a clean oiled bowl, cover with lightly oiled plastic wrap, and leave in a warm place to rise for about 45 minutes or until doubled in size.

3 Increase the oven temperature to 425°F. Transfer the dough to a floured surface and knead lightly to knock out any air. Divide into 2 and roll out to into 2 rounds, about ½–1 inch thick. Transfer to floured baking sheets. Spread the tapenade over the center of each, leaving a border around the edges, then top with the tomatoes, onion, and mozzarella. Drizzle with the remaining olive oil.

4 Loosely cover with plastic wrap and leave to rise for 15 minutes until puffy. Bake for 15–20 minutes, or until the cheese is golden and bubbling and the dough crisp. Scatter with the arugula and Parmesan, drizzle with a little olive oil, and serve.

Making bread to trade
WfWI baking class, DRC

"We are all in this together. We are all responsible. We can all do something to make the world we leave a better place than when we arrived."
Greg Wise

Thai fish curry

5–6 garlic cloves

1-inch piece fresh ginger, peeled

½ cup fresh cilantro

1 fresh or dried red chile

1 tablespoon sesame oil

14oz can chopped tomatoes

14oz can coconut milk

2 cups chicken stock

1 teaspoon Chinese five-spice powder

1 tablespoon nam pla (fish sauce)

1 lb firm white fish, salmon, or shellfish, cut into 1-inch cubes

4oz bean sprouts

4oz water chestnuts

4oz bamboo shoots

1 lime, cut into wedges

salt

Even my 10-year-old daughter loves this—it's a real mix of fresh, canned, and even frozen ingredients. Is it a stew? Is it a soup? I don't know... I used to be more of a purist, trying to find authentic ingredients – now, I cheat like crazy and you really can't tell the difference. You can throw this together in half an hour, but it's best made the day before as it gives all the flavors time to do their thing. We probably eat this at least once every 10 days—a real family favorite!

Prepare 10 minutes | **Cook** 25 minutes | **Serves** 4

1 Add the garlic, ginger, cilantro, chile, sesame oil, tomatoes, and a little salt to a food processor or blender and process until smooth.

2 Pour the blended mixture into a large heavy-bottomed pan over medium heat. Cook for 5 minutes or until the garlic and ginger are softened, stirring frequently. Pour in the coconut milk and chicken stock. Stir in the five spice powder and the nam pla and bring to a boil.

3 Add the fish or shellfish and cook for 3–5 minutes, or until cooked through. Stir in the bean sprouts, water chestnuts, and bamboo shoots and cook for another 1–2 minutes or until softened. Serve with lime wedges and rice or thin rice noodles.

"What if one doesn't know what it feels like to lose a home in the middle of the night while you were sleeping in your own bed? Or to be forced to walk for days and weeks in the middle of the forest without any food to save your life and that of your loved ones? What then? Is that a free pass to ignore, to pretend, to do nothing?"

Lisa Shannon

Roast vegetables with peanut sauce

4 tablespoons canola oil

2 garlic cloves, crushed

1 teaspoon coriander seeds

1 teaspoon cumin seeds

2 eggplants, cut into 1-inch cubes

2 zucchini, cut into 1-inch cubes

2 red onions, cut into wedges

8oz squash, cut into 1-inch cubes

2 teaspoons honey

4 tablespoons fresh mint leaves

4 tablespoons fresh cilantro leaves

2 scallions, sliced

juice of 1 lime

For the peanut sauce

1 tablespoon canola oil

1 small onion, finely chopped

1–2 garlic cloves, crushed

1-inch piece fresh ginger, peeled and grated

1 teaspoon tamari or soy sauce

1 tablespoon lemon juice

2–3 tablespoons smooth peanut butter

2 teaspoons sugar, or to taste

I have made this peanut sauce over an open charcoal fire stove in remote LRA- (Lord's Resistance Army-) affected Dungu, in the Congo, simply using salt instead of tamari. My host family loved it and make it now as a staple. It may seem like a lot of ingredients, but it is super-quick and easy to make.

Prepare 25 minutes | **Cook** 35 minutes | **Serves** 4

1 Preheat the oven to 400°F. To make the roasted vegetables, place the oil, garlic, coriander, cumin, eggplant, zucchini, onions, squash, and honey into a large bowl. Stir to combine and season. Pour the mixture onto a large baking sheet and cook in the oven for 30–35 minutes, or until tender, stirring once halfway through cooking.

2 Meanwhile, make the peanut sauce. Heat the oil in a frying pan over medium heat and cook the onion for 1–2 minutes, or until softened. Add the garlic and ginger and cook for another minute before stirring in the tamari or soy sauce, lemon juice, peanut butter, and 1 cup water. Add sugar to taste. Simmer for 3–4 minutes, then set aside to cool.

3 Remove the vegetables from the oven and sprinkle with the mint, cilantro, and scallions. Squeeze on the lime juice and serve with the peanut sauce.

"The greatest gift is to see the impact of our work in local communities and to see young people getting excited about being agents of positive change for the future."
Craig Kielburger

Kachumbari salad

1 lb firm and ripe tomatoes, sliced or diced
1–1½ red onions, very thinly sliced
4 tablespoons fresh cilantro, chopped
¼ cup extra virgin olive oil
1 chile, sliced (optional)
1–2 tablespoons lemon or lime juice
salt and freshly ground black pepper

A classic Kenyan dish, Kachumbari is one of my all-time favorite salads. I first tried it during a trip to one of Free The Children's communities in the Maasai Mara. The fresh local ingredients make this a healthy side dish for grilled meats, chicken, or fish, and come together to create a tasty treat that would satisfy any Maasai warrior. Kachumbari is best served cold, either plain or with warm chapati. I enjoy the dish for its boost of nutrients and Kenyan flair.

Prepare 5 minutes | **Serves** 4

1 Place the tomatoes into a medium salad bowl with the onions. Stir in the chopped cilantro.

2 Drizzle with the olive oil and stir in the chile, if using. Season and gradually add the lemon or lime juice to taste.

Cook's tip

If you prefer a milder onion flavor, rinse the onion slices in hot salty water before putting them in the salad. This will ensure the onion is less harsh on the palate. Squeeze the lemon or lime juice into the salad just before serving to avoid sogginess. If the tomato and onion are chopped more finely, this recipe also works well as a homemade salsa.

> *"The knowledge of food drives my humanitarian consciousness.*
> *It's not about distant communities, but rather the comment on your doorstep.*
> *I think local, to drive global change."*

Arthur Potts Dawson

Roasted eggplant tower with spinach and tomato

2 large or 4 small eggplants,
sliced into 1-inch slices
1 lb spinach, washed
¹⁄₃ cup olive oil
8oz halloumi cheese, sliced
juice of 1 lemon
2½ cups arugula
salt

For the tomato sauce
1 tablespoon olive oil
½ onion, chopped
2 garlic cloves, crushed
14oz can chopped tomatoes
½ teaspoon dried oregano
pinch of red pepper flakes
(optional)
salt and freshly ground
black pepper

A perfect example of relationships between textures and flavors. Eggplant and tomato are a wonderful marriage, and the halloumi brings in a texture and flavor that sets the dish off, allowing each ingredient to show off its individual character.

Prepare 10 minutes, plus 20 minutes salting | **Cook** 40 minutes | **Serves** 4–6

1 Lightly salt each eggplant slice and arrange in a colander. Set aside for 20 minutes.

2 Meanwhile, make the tomato sauce. Heat the olive oil in a large pan over medium heat and cook the onion for 2–3 minutes, or until beginning to soften. Add the garlic and cook for another minute. Stir in the chopped tomatoes, oregano, and red pepper flakes (if using) and season. Simmer for 15 minutes, then process using a stick blender until smooth.

3 Preheat the oven to 350°F. Cook the spinach in boiling salted water for 1 minute or until wilted, then drain thoroughly. Drizzle with a little of the olive oil and set aside to cool.

4 Pat the eggplant slices dry using paper towels. Heat a little of the olive oil in a frying pan over medium heat and cook the eggplant in batches for 1–2 minutes on each side, or until golden brown. Transfer to a plate lined with paper towels.

5 Now make the towers. Place an eggplant slice onto a baking sheet, and arrange some of the cooked spinach over the top. Spoon a little tomato sauce onto the spinach, covering it completely. Top with another eggplant slice and repeat. Add a slice of halloumi cheese to the top. Repeat to make 4–6 towers, reserving a little of the tomato sauce.

6 Cook in the oven for 15 minutes, or until the cheese is golden and crisp. Dress the arugula with the remaining olive oil and the lemon juice, then arrange a handful of arugula on top of each tower. Spoon a little tomato sauce around the base of each tower and serve.

"I have been working with local farmers for over 25 years and I have the utmost respect and admiration for them—they are the only folks I know that work harder and longer than chefs!"

Susan Spicer

Sautéed fish with cucumbers, pineapple and chiles

1 medium cucumber, peeled

1 cup pineapple, peeled and cut into 2-inch dice

juice of 2 limes

2 tablespoons palm or brown sugar

2 tablespoons nam pla (fish sauce)

1-inch piece fresh ginger, peeled and grated

2 teaspoons minced or grated lemongrass

2 fresh Thai chiles or ½ teaspoon sambal oelek (red chile paste)

4 × 6oz fillets of firm, white sustainable fish, such as seabass, cod or haddock

2 teaspoons canola oil

2 tablespoons chopped fresh herbs, such as cilantro, basil, and mint

salt and freshly ground black pepper

This versatile dish can be prepared with any firm, white fish you fancy. It's particularly good with sea bass, cod or haddock.

Prepare 15 minutes | **Cook** 10 minutes | **Serves** 4

1 Cut the cucumber lengthwise into four pieces, then remove and discard the seeds. Slice the cucumber and place in a bowl with the pineapple. Set aside.

2 Mix the lime juice with the sugar, fish sauce, ginger, lemongrass and chiles in a small bowl and stir until the sugar is dissolved. Pour over the cucumbers and pineapple and stir. Set aside.

3 Season the fish fillets. Heat the oil in a frying pan over high heat to the sizzling point and add the fish, skin-side up. Reduce the heat to medium and cook for 4 minutes, then turn and cook for 2 minutes or until cooked through. Transfer to four serving plates and top with the cucumber and pineapple mixture. Sprinkle with the herbs, and serve with steamed rice or rice noodles.

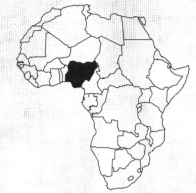

NIGERIA

Average WfWI participant

Age: 41-50

Married: 75% / Widowed: 21% / Single: 4%

Children: 4 / No. in household: 9

Literate: 42% / No formal education: 32%

Chichima's Story

Despite the 1999 Constitution giving equal rights to all, regardless of gender, Nigeria's legal system has resulted in widespread unequal treatment of women. Women for Women International's Nigeria program aims to teach women that they are, in fact, equal to men, and that the education of their daughters is as important as that of their sons.

Chichima has two children-Abaeze, her 11-year old son, and Lolade, her 8-year old daughter. Before joining Women for Women International, Chichima was a peasant farmer, struggling to support her children.

"When I was young, many girls did not go to school. Parents believed that when girls have a good education they do not respect their husbands, and so men will be afraid of seeking their hand in marriage. Knowledge is power-I have always known this. I was studying for my teaching certificate while looking after my children, but then my husband left us and our lives changed. We moved in with my parents, my father was very sick, and I had to work to feed Abaeze and Lolade, so I started growing cassava to sell in the market.

Through WfWI I trained in farming skills, and learned how to get a better yield from the land. I started making fried garri to sell at the market, and with the allowance from my sponsor I was able to resume my teacher training. Now I teach at a nursery school in the village. I also teach women in the village to read and write, and I am educating them about the consequences of female genital cutting.

I used some of my savings and borrowed some money to build a two-bedroom mud house. There was enough money left over to buy two large coolers, which I rent out, and a large container for saving water in the rainy season. I continue to garden, growing food to feed my family, and what we don't eat my children sell at the market. I am proud that I can take care of our needs. I have begun saving for Abaeze to go someday to job skills training in medicine. Lolade wants to know if she can be a teacher like me when she grows up, and I tell her, 'Yes!' Together we will give women back their power.

When I joined WfWI, a bad aura left my life and the joy of living came back to me. Here, each woman has liberty to express herself and equally hear other women's stories. I worry less now-I set goals and I plan to achieve them."

NIGERIA

Population: 170,123,740

Square km: 923,768

GDP per capita: $2,600

Unemployment: 21%

Life expectancy:
Female : 55 years / Male:49 years

Conflict dates: 1999-present

Total no. killed: 13,500 (estimated)

Recipes from Nigeria

With a huge land mass and fertile soil, Nigeria has the resources to become a major food provider on the African continent. It grows more cassava (also called yuca and manioc) than any other country in the world, and the tube-shaped root, which can be processed into many different flours, chips and syrups, is eaten by an estimated 100 million Nigerians-two-thirds of the population-at least once a day.

Nigeria is comprised of hundreds of ethnic groups, 70 percent of whom are involved in subsistence farming. The country cuts across a range of natural geographic zones, including the Sahara Desert, the green savannah and the tropical rainforest. With such a hugely diverse range of crop possibilities and soil, it is not surprising that Nigerian cuisine is equally expansive. Tropical fruits such as oranges, tangerines, mangoes, pawpaw, African bread fruit, banana and bush mango all feature, and spices and herbs such as pepper seeds, chiles, garlic, cayenne, turmeric and bitter leaf, together with palm and groundnut oil, are used to create richly-flavored soups and sauces. Festive meals in particular tend to be colorful and lavish.

Ukpo ogede

This is a steamed savory pudding made from over-ripe plantains mixed with plaintain flour, crawfish and onions, spooned into parcels and steamed before serving, and eaten on its own or as an accompaniment with cornmeal pap (porridge).

Prepare 15 minutes | **Cook** 1 hour | **Serves** 6

1-1¼ cups plantain flour
5 over-ripe plantains, washed
2-3 teaspoons ground dried crawfish (optional)
1 onion, chopped
3 tablespoons palm oil
2 vegetable stock cubes, crumbled
salt and freshly ground black pepper

1 Sieve the plantain flour into a bowl, add a little warm water and mix to form a thick and stiff but smooth paste.
2 Peel and mash or finely chop the plantains and blend into the paste. Then stir in the dry crawfish (if using) and onion. Mix in the palm oil and stock cubes and season generously. If the mixture seems too stiff add a little extra warm water, or add a little extra plantain flour if it is too soft. It should be very thick and stiff but a just stirrable consistency.
3 Spoon the mixture into small parcels of foil, ramekins or banana leaves, sealed well with foil. Place in a steamer over a pan of simmering water and steam for 40-60 minutes, or until cooked thorough. Serve with pap or on its own as a snack.

Beef and okra soup

This soup is so simple and quick to make. Once the meat is tender, add the okra-it cooks really quickly.

Prepare 15 minutes | **Cook** 40 minutes | **Serves** 5-6

1 lb beef, thinly sliced
½ medium onion, chopped
1lb okra, sliced
2 tablespoons dried crawfish (optional)
1 teaspoon dried red chile, powdered or crushed (or optional, chopped or ground red pepper)
2 tablespoons red palm oil
4oz spinach, chopped
salt and freshly ground black pepper

1 Place the beef in a pan with 4 cups water. Add the onion and crawfish powder, if using. Bring to a boil and simmer for 25-30 minutes.
2 Stir in the okra with the remaining ingredients. Cook for another 10 minutes, stirring continuously.
3 Serve with pounded yam or pounded cassava.

"The capacity of a human being to survive in adversity inspires me to do my work with refugees. It makes what I do more than a treat—it's very rewarding."

Tindyebwa Agaba

Beef stroganoff

1 lb top round steak, sliced into very thin strips

1 teaspoon paprika, plus extra for sprinkling

4 tablespoons unsalted butter

2 tablespoons olive oil

1 large onion, sliced

10oz crimini mushrooms, sliced

3 tablespoons whiskey

½–1 beef stock cube

³/₄ cup sour cream

¹/₃ cup flat-leaf parsley, chopped (optional)

salt and freshly ground black pepper

tagliatelle, to serve

I love this recipe because it reminds me of my mother, who cooks it for us at home in Scotland. We gorge on it around winter fires and there never seems to be enough!

Prepare 15 minutes | **Cook** 25 minutes | **Serves** 4

1 Place the steak in a shallow bowl and season with salt, a generous amount of freshly ground black pepper, and the paprika. Toss well to coat evenly, then set aside.

2 In a large frying pan, heat half the butter and oil, add the onion, and cook for 2–3 minutes until softened, then stir in the mushrooms and cook for another 4–5 minutes.

3 Using a slotted spoon, remove the mushroom and onion mixture and place on a plate. Heat the remaining butter and oil in the pan until very hot, then cook the beef for 2–3 minutes until lightly browned.

4 Return the onions and mushrooms to the pan and add the whiskey. Dissolve the beef stock cube in ¹/₂ cup boiling water and pour into the pan. Cook for 1–2 minutes, then stir in the sour cream, return to the heat, and gently heat through. Simmer over low heat for 5–10 minutes (take care not to let it boil or it will curdle), then season to taste. Sprinkle with a little more paprika and the chopped parsley (if using). Serve immediately with cooked tagliatelle.

"My hope is to plant the seeds for a lifetime of positive eating habits and enjoyment of food."

Stephanie Alexander

Stephanie Alexander: Mary's rabbit pie

1 wild rabbit
8 cups chicken stock or water
1 rib celery, sliced
½ carrot, sliced
1 onion, chopped
zest of 1 lemon
1 stalk parsley, plus 2 tablespoons, chopped
1 bay leaf
1 sprig thyme
1 teaspoon black peppercorns
1 tablespoon olive oil
4oz bacon, finely chopped
8oz button mushrooms, sliced
½ cup sliced almonds, toasted
1 disk prepared pie dough
⅓ cup bread crumbs
2 tablespoons melted butter
salt and freshly ground black pepper

For the sauce
10 tablespoons butter
1¼ cup all-purpose flour
⅔ cup heavy cream
juice of 1 lemon

Mary was my mother, and this rabbit pie is a family heirloom, cooked whenever my family meets. It features as part of my sister's pre-Christmas lunch gathering, and is requested by our children if a picnic is planned. In my family this pie was always cooked in a rectangular pan and the pie cut into squares. It could also be cooked in a 9- or 10-inch loose-bottomed round tart pan and be cut into wedges.

Prepare 30 minutes | **Cook** 3 hours 10 minutes | **Serves** 8

1 Remove the kidneys and liver from the rabbit and reserve. Add the rabbit to a large pan over medium heat and pour in the stock or water. Add the celery, carrot, onion, lemon zest, herbs (except for the chopped parsley), and peppercorns. Bring to a simmer and cook for 1½–2 hours or until the back legs of the rabbit are tender. Remove from the heat and allow the rabbit to cool completely in the stock. Remove the rabbit, strain the cooking liquid, and reserve. Strip the meat from the carcass, cut into small pieces, and place in a bowl. Discard the bones.

2 Heat the olive oil in a frying pan over medium heat and add the bacon and mushrooms. Cook for 5 minutes or until the bacon is cooked, remove from the pan, and add to the rabbit. Add the reserved kidneys and liver to the pan and cook briefly to sear. Roughly chop the kidneys and liver and add to the bowl along with the almonds and chopped parsley. Season well and mix to combine. Cover the bowl with plastic wrap and chill.

3 To make the sauce, melt the butter in the frying pan over low heat and stir in the flour to make a roux. Gradually stir in 5 cups of the reserved cooking liquid, increase the heat to medium, and bring to a simmer. Add the cream and lemon juice and simmer for 10 minutes. Season to taste, cool, and then add enough sauce to the bowl of rabbit mixture to make a creamy but not sloppy filling—you might not need it all.

4 Preheat the oven to 400°F. Line a 11 x 7 x 2-inch pan with the pie dough (reserve some dough to make a latticed top) then line with parchment paper. Fill with baking beans and bake blind for 20 minutes. Remove the baking beans and allow to cool.

5 Reduce oven temperature to 350°F. Spoon the rabbit filling into the pie crust. Scatter the top with the bread crumbs and drizzle with the melted butter. Top the pie with the reserved dough in a lattice pattern. Bake in the oven for 20–30 minutes or until the dough is well browned and the bread crumbs are golden. Serve at room temperature or cold, with chutney or cornichons.

Cook's tip

I have also made the pie with chicken thighs, and on one occasion with leftover Thanksgiving or Christmas turkey. If using one of these alternatives, ensure that the meat is moist. It may mean gently simmering the cooked meat in a little stock before folding it into the sauce.

"I am a big advocate of pure, wholesome food—I truly believe that if everyone were to eat nutritious foods, we would be on our way to solving our collective health and environmental problems and safeguarding the Earth for its future inhabitants."

Nora Pouillon

Baked fish with three-colored peppers

4 teaspoons olive oil

1 medium onion, thinly sliced

2 garlic cloves, crushed

2 green peppers, seeded and cut into thin strips

1 red pepper, seeded and cut into thin strips

1 yellow pepper, seeded and cut into thin strips

1 cup white wine

2–3 tablespoons chopped mixed fresh herbs, such as thyme, oregano, and rosemary, plus a few small sprigs to garnish

1½ lbs firm white fish fillet, such as halibut, cut into 4 portions

16–20 baby new potatoes

This meal is nutritious and easy to prepare, and the quantities can easily be doubled or even tripled to feed a large crowd. You can use any fish (or even chicken breasts), but I like to use halibut because it's both wild and sustainable—we source ours at Restaurant Nora from Alaska—but it has a tendency to be dry. That's why I like to roast or bake it with vegetables plus some liquid and season it with olive oil and herbs.

Prepare 10 minutes | **Cook** 15 minutes | **Serves** 4

1 Preheat the oven to 425°F. Heat half of the olive oil in a frying pan over medium heat. Add the onion, garlic, and peppers and cook for 5 minutes or until softened, stirring frequently. Add the wine and chopped herbs and season to taste. Bring to a boil and cook for 1 minute, stirring to combine. Remove the pan from the heat.

2 Spoon the pepper mixture and juices into a baking dish large enough to accommodate the fish in one layer. Arrange the fish fillets on top. Drizzle with the remaining olive oil and season to taste. Bake in the oven for 8–10 minutes, or until the fish is cooked through.

3 Meanwhile, steam or boil the potatoes for 10–15 minutes, or until a fork can be easily inserted.

4 Use a spatula to transfer each fish fillet with the pepper mixture and juices to the center of four large, warm, dinner plates. Surround the fish with the potatoes, and garnish with the fresh herbs before serving.

"Cooking and gardening are two of the best ways to encourage good health and self reliance—anything we can do to share our passion for these wonderful endeavours is what motivates us."

Greg Higgins

Curried stew of sweet potatoes, pinto beans and cabbage

2 ¹/₃ cups pinto beans
3–4 tablespoons olive oil
1 onion, chopped
4 garlic cloves, crushed
1-inch piece of fresh ginger, peeled and grated
2 tablespoons Madras curry powder
1 tablespoon garam masala
8 cups vegetable stock or water
1 cup sweet potato, peeled and cut into ½-inch cubes
1 red pepper, seeded and cut into ½-inch cubes
4 cups cabbage, chopped
½ cup sliced almonds, toasted

This is a typical vegetarian dish that we cook at our restaurant Higgins. My wife is a vegetarian, and we cook this at home as well, using vegetables from our organic garden. Curries are great in any season, but we love them in the autumn and winter to warm us and complement the rich flavors of the season's vegetables. This stew is hearty and warming on a brisk winter day—try jazzing it up with some fresh chile or a squeeze of fresh lime and a spoonful of yogurt.

Prepare 15 minutes, plus overnight soaking | **Cook** 2 hours | **Serves** 4

1 Begin the night before. Place the beans in a bowl, cover with cold water and leave to soak overnight.
2 The next day, heat the olive oil in a heavy-bottomed saucepan over medium heat. Add the onions, garlic, ginger, curry powder, and garam masala and cook for 3–4 minutes, or until the onions are just beginning to soften.
3 Drain the soaked beans and add to the pan, followed by the stock or water. Bring to a gentle simmer and cook for 1–1½ hours, or until the beans are just tender, stirring occasionally and adding more water if needed.
4 Add the sweet potato, red pepper, and cabbage. Season generously and simmer for another 15–20 minutes, or until the sweet potato is tender. Serve in bowls with a sprinkle of almonds, accompanied by a loaf of crusty bread and a salad.

WfWI Bosnia participants and graduates gather to exhibit and sell their produce. These meetings not only provide an opportunity to trade, but also strengthen relationships within the community.

> *"I am inspired by the idea of promoting nutritious, wholesome food, and the need to eliminate starvation."*
>
> **Peter Davis**

Braised goat or lamb with greens and corn

6 garlic cloves, chopped

½ cup lime juice

2 cups olive oil

5 lbs leg of goat or lamb

3 onions, chopped

2 carrots, chopped

2 ribs celery, chopped

4 hot chiles, chopped

4 cups chicken stock

4 ears of corn, peeled and kernels removed

8oz spring or collard greens, trimmed of stems and thinly sliced

salt and freshly ground black pepper

Prepare 10 minutes, plus marinating | **Cook** 5½ hours | **Serves** 4

1 The day before serving, mix the garlic with the lime juice and 1¹/₂ cups of the olive oil in a large dish. Add the goat or lamb and turn to coat. Cover with plastic wrap and leave in the fridge to marinate overnight.

2 Preheat the broiler to medium. Remove the meat from the marinade and broil for 10–15 minutes, or until browned on all sides. Meanwhile, heat the remaining oil in a large, lidded heavy-bottomed pan over medium heat. Add the onions, carrots, celery, and chiles and cook for 5–6 minutes, or until lightly browned. Then add the meat.

3 Pour in the chicken stock, and bring to a boil. Reduce the heat to a slow simmer and cover. Cook for 4–5 hours, or until the meat is very tender and pulls away from the bone easily. Transfer the meat to a plate, cover and keep warm. Strain the cooking liquid and return to the pan. Pull the meat from the bone and discard the bone.

4 Return the pan to the heat. Bring to a boil and boil rapidly until the liquid has reduced by half, then add the corn, greens, and pulled meat. Simmer for 20 minutes. Serve with rice.

"Having children has certainly inspired me to become more involved in charity and other humanitarian projects. Setting a good example for them and passing the inspiration forward has been a large motivation."

René Redzepi

Simple cucumber fermentation

1 lb organic medium-sized
cucumbers, chopped
1 tablespoon salt
1 tablespoon balsamic apple
vinegar
4oz fresh dill, including stalks
1 tablespoon juniper berries,
crushed
4oz horseradish, peeled and
cut into ribbons
1 lb organic baby
cucumbers

To serve

20 nasturtium leaves
28 chamomile buds
40 white currants
1½ cups buttermilk
½ teaspoon cold-pressed
canola oil

Lactic fermentation is an increasingly important part of our repertoire at Noma. The ability to naturally accentuate the flavor of carefully grown produce is of great interest to us. The lovely intense sour and salinity that this process provides is an excellent counterbalance to any dish or serving. Although this is an example of a relatively simple lactic fermentation, there are endless permutations to this technique. For instance, in adjusting the flavor of a new blueberry dessert, we use both lactic-fermented wild blueberries and fresh ones, thus calibrating the acidity and adding another facet of the dark forest flavors.

Prepare 10 minutes, plus fermentation time of 5 days | **Serves** 4

1 Process the medium-sized cucumbers, salt, vinegar, dill, juniper, and horseradish in a food processor or blender to form a purée.
2 Place the baby cucumbers in a nonreactive airtight container with the puréed mixture and allow to ferment at room temperature (ideally 70°F) for 5 days.
3 Wash the nasturtium leaves and chamomile buds in iced water then dry in a salad spinner. Pack into plastic containers and store on ice until needed.
4 Serve the fermented baby cucumbers garnished with the nasturtium leaves, chamomile buds, and whitecurrants, and drizzled with the buttermilk and oil.

community 169

*"I'm helping to create an economic system that will respect and protect the Earth—
one that would establish a global network of local living economies.
Business is beautiful when it's a vehicle for serving the common good."*

Judy Wicks

Sautéed chicken and mushrooms in a Marsala and sage sauce

4 boneless, skinless chicken breasts, halved
all-purpose flour, for coating
2 tablespoons olive oil
2 tablespoons unsalted butter
2 small shallots, chopped
1–2 garlic cloves, crushed
1 ½ cups crimini or button mushrooms, sliced
¼ cup dry Marsala
1 cup chicken stock
2 tablespoons butter, chilled and diced (optional)
2 tablespoons chopped fresh sage
1 teaspoon soy sauce
salt and freshly ground black pepper

This recipe is from the *White Dog Cafe Cookbook*, which I co-authored with Chef Kevin von Klause. Although it can be made with whole chicken breasts, the medallions give more surface area to drench with the luscious sauce.

Prepare 15 minutes | **Cook** 20 minutes | **Serves** 4

1 Place each chicken breast half between 2 sheets of plastic wrap and pound with a meat tenderizer or a rolling pin until very thin. Cut each flattened piece into 3 or 4 medallions. Season each medallion and dip both sides into the flour to coat.

2 Heat the olive oil in a large frying pan over medium-high heat. Cook the chicken medallions, in batches if necessary, for 1 minute on each side, or until lightly browned and cooked through. Transfer to a plate and loosely cover with foil to keep warm.

3 Add the unsalted butter to the pan and melt over a medium heat. Add the shallots and cook for 1 minute. Add the garlic and cook for 1–2 minutes. Add the mushrooms and ¼ teaspoon salt, and cook for 4 minutes or until the mushrooms are softened. Spoon the mushrooms out onto a plate and keep warm.

4 Add the Marsala to the pan, bring to a boil, and cook until reduced by half. Pour in the chicken stock and add the chilled butter cubes (if using). Cook for 5–10 minutes or until the sauce reaches a consistency that will coat the back of a spoon. Return the mushrooms to the pan and remove from the heat. Stir in the sage and soy sauce. Serve the chicken on warmed plates with the sauce spooned over.

KOSOVO

Average WfWI participant

Age: 31-40

Married: 76% / Widowed: 3% / Single: 21%

Children: 2 / No. in household: 7

Literate: 92% / No formal education: 7%

Sylbije's story

Although the Serbian government claimed it was only looking for terrorists, many Kosovan-Albanians were the target of Serb aggression in the late 1990s. The house where Sylbije lived with her husband and children just outside Pristina was very close to a Serbian police checkpoint. Both of Albanian descent, she and her husband feared for their lives and the lives of their children.

"During the war, we decided that I would flee without my husband, and take our children into the mountains. This was our only chance for safety. Eventually, we made it to Germany and found my uncle, who sheltered us for nearly a year. After the war was over we returned home and found that my husband had been killed by the Serbs. The only way I could survive was to sell the clothes that people had given me while we were living in Germany. I began growing seedlings and sold them anywhere I could.

I heard about the WfWI program and wanted to participate. Even though I lived 15 miles from where the training was being held, I was determined to do it. I chose the cooking course. I learned so much and began to take part in different fairs and markets, selling what I was learning to make. Now, customers know me and like to buy my pastries and breads. There are so many vendors in the markets, but I have my own customers who come to the market for what I make and want to buy only from me. I have started my own small company and have hired other women to work with me and we work together to sell our food.

My sponsor saved my life. Because of her, I was able to meet other women and to gain so much knowledge. I had to quit school after I finished the 7th grade because my parents couldn't afford to pay for the expenses, but I want my children to be successful in life. I can be sure they will stay in school and achieve their goals."

KOSOVO

Population: 1,836,529

Square km: 10,887

GDP per capita: $6,500

Unemployment: 45%

Conflict dates: 1998–1999

Total no. killed: 21,500+ (estimated)

Estimated military deaths:
3,800–8,000 insurgents

Estimated civilian deaths: 527 (estimated);
13,000 Kosovan Albanians

Internally displaced persons: 18,000

Recipes from Kosovo

Formerly part of Yugoslavia, Kosovo is Europe's youngest country and one of its poorest. Its food has been heavily influenced by the country's Albanian inhabitants, who comprise well over 75 percent of the population, but also by its neighbors, Turkey, Greece, Serbia, and Italy. Fare is generally simple and hearty, often consisting of meat and potatoes or rice. Because of its harsh continental climate, vegetables are largely seasonal. Cucumbers, green tomatoes, cabbages and peppers are abundant in the warmer months and following the summer harvest are often jarred and canned for later consumption or for selling at local markets. Beef, lamb, and chicken are common, but despite many freshwater lakes in Kosovo, very little fish is eaten. Dairy products-from both cows and sheep-are made locally and served fresh. When available, meals are finished with apples, cherries, pears, quince, or wild berries.

Sarma

Pickled cabbage or vine leaves enveloping a combination of seasoned ground meat and cooked rice, perfect for serving as an appetizer.

Prepare 30 minutes | **Cook** 1 hour 5 minutes | **Makes** 14 leaves for appetizers

1 tablespoon vegetable oil
1 onion, chopped
½ cup cooked rice
1 lb ground veal or beef
14 large pickled cabbage or vine leaves

1 Heat the vegetable oil and cook the onion until softened. Remove from the heat and add the rice, meat, and salt and pepper, taking care not to add too much salt as the leaves are quite salty. Stir everything well until thoroughly combined.
2 Place a spoonful of the mixture into the center of each leaf, then wrap the sides of each leaf around to cover the mixture. Place in a pan. Once all the meat is wrapped and in the pan, cover the surface with smaller leaves and pour in just enough water to cover. Bring to a gentle simmer and cook on low heat for about 1 hour. (If you prefer, you can arrange the leaves in a roasting pan, bring to a boil on the stove and transfer to a preheated 350° F oven for 30 minutes).

Savory semolina cake

Dense and moist, this semolina cake is flavored with softened leek and served in sesame seed-topped slices.

Prepare 10 minutes | **Cook** 30 minutes | **Serves** 6-8

2 cups fine semolina
3 eggs
³/₄ cup vegetable oil
2 cups Quark or cottage cheese
½ cup sour cream
1 teaspoon baking powder
handful of finely chopped leek (or spinach or nettle leaves)
½ teaspoon salt
1 tablespoon sesame seeds

1 Preheat the oven to 400° F. Grease a 8-inch round cake pan and line with parchment paper. Place all the ingredients except the sesame seeds in a large mixing bowl, and mix together until well combined and with a soft but not runny consistency.
2 Pour into the prepared cake pan, and scatter the top with the sesame seeds. Bake in the oven for 30 minutes, until the pie is golden and cooked through.

"When peace returned we replanted our gardens and orchards, tending them with great care and gratitude."

WfWI Bosnia and Herzegovina participant

Cherry compote

Prepare 15 minutes, plus 1 week maturing
Cook 5 minutes
Makes about 26oz

1 cup brandy
⅓ cup sugar
1 lb cherries, pitted

1 Pour the brandy into a small saucepan over low heat. Add the sugar and ⅓ cup water. Heat gently until the sugar has dissolved.

2 Meanwhile, pack the cherries into a large, sterilized glass jar. Pour the warm brandy liquid over the cherries, making sure the fruit is totally submerged in the alcohol. Seal and store in a cool dark place for a week to allow the flavors to develop, then store in the fridge and use within 2 months. Serve either at room temperature or gently warmed in a pan and spooned over vanilla ice cream.

"You can still be entrepeneurial even if you are poor and have no money."

Esther, WfWI Rwanda participant

Fraser Doherty: Easy jam-filled cookies

2 sticks butter, softened
½ cup sugar
1 teaspoon vanilla extract
2¼ cups all-purpose flour, sifted
½ teaspoon baking powder, sifted
8 tablespoons jam of your choice

Ever since I was a small kid, I have loved cooking—especially baking cakes and making jam! Back when my Gran originally made jam, she would take it, along with scones and cakes, to nursing homes in her Glasgow neighborhood and share afternoon tea with the residents. I've taken her act of kindness as my inspiration to conduct hundreds of free tea parties all over Scotland for elderly people.

Prepare 15 minutes | **Cook** 20 minutes | **Makes** 30

1 Preheat the oven to 350°F. Line 2 large baking sheets with parchment paper Place the butter and sugar in a mixing bowl and beat until pale and fluffy.
2 Add the vanilla extract and continue beating until well combined. Using a metal spoon, fold in the flour and baking powder until the mixture forms a soft dough.
3 Take a small piece of the dough and roll in your hands to make a ball. Place on the baking sheet. Repeat with the remaining dough, leaving a gap between each one to allow for spread during baking.
4 Using a finger, make an imprint deep enough to hold a little jam into each ball. Carefully fill each cookie with about ½ teaspoon jam, making sure you don't overfill.
5 Cook in the oven for 15–20 minutes, or until lightly golden brown. Carefully transfer to a wire rack to cool completely before eating. The cookies will keep in an airtight container for up to 3 days.

"sharing inspires feelings of unity, belonging, and responsibility. This inspires others to create happiness in their communities, providing everlasting benefits. The best feeling anyone can have is witnessing lives changing for the better."

Zuhal Sultan

Klecha (date and walnut–stuffed cookies)

¼ cup milk
1 teaspoon active dry yeast
½ cup sugar
3½ cups all-purpose flour
2 sticks butter, or 1 cup ghee, at room temperature
¼ cup plain yogurt
2 teaspoons confectioners sugar

For the date filling
2 tablespoons butter
8oz (around 10) soft, pitted Mejool dates, finely chopped
2 teaspoons ground cardamom

For the walnut filling
³/₄ cup walnuts, toasted and finely chopped
1 teaspoon ground cinnamon
3 teaspoons sugar
1 egg white

For the egg wash
1 egg, beaten
2 tablespoons milk

I love this recipe because it reminds me of precious childhood times with my late mother back in Baghdad. A day or two before Eid, she and I would spend hours in the kitchen preparing to make massive amounts of Klecha to share with our friends and neighbors. Making large quantities can be a grueling task, but it's worth it when the first batch is out of the oven—golden, shiny, mouthwateringly fragrant, and piping hot.

Prepare 45 minutes, plus 30 minutes rising | **Cook** 35 minutes | **Makes** 30 (10 date and 20 walnut)

1 Warm the milk, then add the yeast and 2 tablespoons of sugar and let stand for 10 minutes. Meanwhile, thoroughly mix the flour and butter by hand, rubbing the mixture between your palms. Add the yogurt and the yeast mixture and mix until a dough is formed. You might need to dampen your hands occasionally to do this. Place the dough in a bowl, covered with a clean towel, and put in a warm, dark place for about 30 minutes, so that the dough rises slightly.

2 Preheat the oven to 350°F. Line 2 baking sheets with nonstick baking parchment. Make the date filling. Melt the butter in a pan, add the dates with the cardamom, and cook for 3–4 minutes, until they are golden and a paste forms. Leave to cool. Divide the dough in half, then roll half with a rolling pin into a square about 10 x 10 inches. Add the date filling and spread it over the square from one end, leaving roughly a quarter uncovered. Roll from one side, finishing with the un-covered dough, to form a log. Using the rolling pin, lightly and gently flatten the log, then cut it into 1-inch slices. Arrange on one of the prepared baking sheets, beat the eegg and milk together to make an egg wash, and use to glaze. Set aside while preparing the other filling.

3 Make the walnut filling by combining the finely chopped walnuts with the cinnamon, sugar, and egg white and set aside. Roll out the remaining dough and cut it into 20 x 2-inch rounds. Place a scant teaspoon of the walnut mixture in the center of each, slightly dampen one side of the circle, and fold the other half on top. Press lightly with your finger to stick, then using the end of a fork, press on the edges lightly. Alternatively, you can crimp the edge from end to end to create a nice braidlike edge. Arrange on the other prepared baking sheet.

4 Bake in the oven for 25–30 minutes until golden. Sprinkle with confectioners sugar, and serve warm with coffee.

"Every one of your individual efforts makes a difference."
Jamie Oliver

Apple berry pie

For the pie dough
4 cups all-purpose flour,
plus extra for dusting
³/4 cup confectioners sugar
pinch of sea salt
2 sticks plus 2 tablespoons
unsalted butter, chilled
and cut into cubes
3 large eggs
a splash of milk
a small handful of demerara sugar

For the filling:
10 Granny Smith apples, peeled,
cored and halved, 3 sliced
juice and zest of 2 oranges
7 heaping tablespoons sugar
2³/4 cups (14oz) huckleberries or
blueberries
1 heaping tablespoon
all-purpose flour
1 large egg

Even though it has a strong British heritage, America has embraced the apple pie to the point that it's now considered a quintessentially American dessert. The crumble-like topping sprinkled over my pie is an idea I've been playing around with, and I think it helps make it unique. If you can't find huckleberries, feel free to use fresh or frozen blueberries in their place for equally delicious results.

Prepare 30 minutes, plus resting time | **Cook** 1 hour 5 minutes | **Serves** 10–12

1 You can make your pie dough by hand, or simply pulse all the ingredients in a food processor. If making by hand, sift the flour, confectioners sugar, and salt from a height into a large mixing bowl. Use your fingertips to gently work the cubes of butter into the flour and sugar until the mixture resembles bread crumbs. Transfer a handful of this mixture to a separate bowl, rub it between your fingers to get larger crumbs, then put aside. Add 2 of the eggs and the milk to the main mixture and gently work it together until you have a ball of pie dough. Don't work it too much at this stage—you want to keep it crumbly. Sprinkle a little flour over the dough, then wrap it in plastic wrap and pop it into the fridge to rest for 1 hour.

2 Meanwhile, make the filling. Put the apples into a large pan with the juice and zest of 1 orange, a splash of water, and 5 tablespoons of the sugar. Cover the pan and simmer on medium heat for 10 minutes, until the apples have softened but still hold their shape. Remove from the heat and leave to cool. Scrunch a handful of the berries in a bowl with the remaining sugar and the juice and zest of your remaining orange. Add the rest of the berries. Toss the cooled apples and their juices in a large bowl with the berries and the flour, then put aside.

3 Preheat your oven to 350°F. Take your ball of pie dough out of the fridge and let it come to room temperature. Get yourself a pie dish around 11 inches in diameter. Flour a clean surface and a rolling pin. Cut off a third of your dough and put that piece to one side. Roll the rest into a circle just over ¹/4 inch thick, dusting with flour as you go. Roll the circle of dough up over your rolling pin, then unroll it over the pie dish. Push it into the sides, letting any excess dough hang over the edge. Pour in the fruit filling. Beat the remaining egg and brush all around the edge of the dough with it. Roll out the smaller ball of dough about ¹/4 inch thick and use your rolling pin to lay it over the top of the pie. Brush it all over with more beaten egg, reserving a little. Sprinkle over the reserved crumble mixture and the demerara sugar.

4 Fold the messy edges of dough hanging over the sides back over the pie, sealing the edge by twisting or crimping it as you like. Brush these folded edges with your remaining beaten egg. Using a small, sharp knife, cut a cross into the middle of the pie. Place on the bottom of the oven and bake for 45–55 minutes, until golden and beautiful. Serve with ice cream or whipped cream.

"I have a lot of love to give. That, ultimately, is why I am here (in DRC). However I divide my day—whether I'm working on policy papers or comforting victims of gang rape—my motivation is love."

Ashley Judd

Chocolate layer slice

For the base
8 tablespoons unsalted butter, plus extra for greasing

1 cup all-purpose flour

³/₄ cup pecans, chopped

For the chocolate layer
1 cup sugar

¹/₃ cup cocoa powder

3 tablespoons all-purpose flour

2 tablespoons cornstarch

pinch of salt

3 large egg yolks

2 cups milk

2 tablespoons unsalted butter or margarine

2 teaspoons vanilla extract

For the cream cheese layer
1 cup heavy cream

³/₄ cup (7oz) cream cheese, at room temperature

1 heaping cup confectioners sugar

For the topping
¹/₂ cup heavy cream

¹/₃ cup pecans, chopped

This recipe is divine—completely irresistible. My family and friends joke that it's "all food groups"—salty, sweet, tangy, crunchy, and smooth. I was filming *Kiss the Girls* in North Carolina in 1997, and my driver's mother made this for me. I remember my good intentions of sharing my fortune with the crew, but after taking one bite in my trailer, I didn't come out until I had eaten nearly half of it! It turns out the lady who made it worked in a geriatric doctor's office and for years traded recipes with older women who came through the doors. She has a stupendous archive of old recipes from the Southern states, and my family thinks this one is the *coup de grâce*. It can be made with a sugar substitute and still tastes completely perfect.

Prepare 40 minutes, plus 3 hours chilling | **Cook** 30 minutes | **Serves** 8–12

1 Preheat the oven to 350°F. Grease and a line an 8-inch square, 2-inch deep cake pan.

2 To make the base, melt the butter in a small pan over low heat, then stir in the flour and mix well before adding the pecans. Pour this mixture into the prepared pan and press down evenly. Bake for 20 minutes or until golden in color. Place the pan on a wire cooling rack and allow to cool.

3 Meanwhile, make the chocolate layer. Stir together the sugar, cocoa powder, all-purpose flour, cornstarch, and salt in a medium saucepan. Gradually whisk in the egg yolks and milk until well blended and smooth. Place over a medium heat and cook, stirring, for 6–10 minutes, or until thickened. Stir in the butter and vanilla extract. Pour into a bowl and cover the surface of the mixture with plastic wrap to stop a skin forming as it cools. Set aside to cool for about 30 minutes.

4 Meanwhile, make the cream cheese layer. Whip the cream until stiff peaks form. In a separate bowl, beat the cream cheese with the confectioners sugar until smooth, then gradually beat the whipped cream into the cream cheese mixture until blended. Spread this mixture over the cooled cooked base.

5 Spoon the cooled chocolate mixture over the cream cheese layer, spreading it evenly. Cover with plastic wrap and chill for at least 3 hours or until firm and chilled throughout.

6 Finally, whip the cream for the topping until stiff peaks form. Spread the cream over the chocolate layer and scatter with the chopped pecans. Carefully lift the cake from the pan and cut into 8–12 squares.

"Unleashing the potential of women and girls is an economic imperative and a critical part of reviving the global economy. I have met so many women entrepreneurs who see business as the path to opportunity – and see themselves as creating hope and possibility."

Gayle Tzemach Lemmon

Baba ganoush (smoked eggplant dip)

2 eggplants, about 1½ lbs
2 garlic cloves, crushed
juice of 1 lemon
2 tablespoons tahini
large pinch of ground cumin
3 tablespoons plain yogurt
(optional)
salt and freshly ground
black pepper
To serve
extra virgin olive oil
chopped fresh flat-leaf parsley

A traditional Middle Eastern dish, delicious served with pita bread, salad, and hummus (below) as part of a mezze meal.

Prepare 10 minutes, plus 30 minutes cooling and draining
| **Cook** 10 minutes | **Serves** 8

1 Preheat the broiler to high. Prick the eggplants with a fork and broil them, turning occasionally, until the skin blisters and blackens all over. When they are cool, peel away the skin and discard. Place the eggplants in a colander and set aside for about 15 minutes to drain off any excess liquid.
2 Put the eggplants into a food processor along with the garlic, lemon juice, tahini, cumin, and yogurt (if using). Process until smooth. Season to taste then spoon into a serving bowl. Drizzle with the oil, sprinkle with the chopped parsley, and serve.

Hummus

14oz can chickpeas,
drained and rinsed
4 tablespoons tahini
2 garlic cloves, crushed
juice of 2 lemons
3 tablespoons extra virgin
olive oil, plus extra for drizzling
pinch of paprika

Prepare 10 minutes | **Serves** 4

1 Place the chickpeas, tahini, garlic, and lemon juice in a food processor and blend until smooth. While the food processor is running, drizzle in the olive oil.
2 Season and spoon into a small bowl. Garnish with a pinch of paprika and a drizzle of olive oil.

Serving suggestion
Serve with warm pita bread drizzled with a little olive oil and zaatar. Alternatively, this is perfect as a summer sandwich filling: spread generously over a slice of whole-wheat bread, topped with fresh spinach leaves.

"Poverty is not created by poor people. It is not their fault that they are poor. Poverty is created by the system, imposed on good-blooded human beings, but we can peel it off. Today almost two-thirds of the world's population are rejected by the conventional banking system through no fault of their own. Banks tell us that we are not credit-worthy, but shouldn't it be the other way round? We should be deciding whether the banks are people-worthy."

Muhammad Yunus

Piaju (spicy lentil and onion fritters)

These tasty fritters are a great party snack, and are especially popular at Ramadan. Perfect for sharing.

Prepare 20 minutes, plus 30 minutes soaking | **Cook** 8–10 minutes | **Makes** 18–20

¾ cup dried red lentils
2-inch piece of fresh ginger, peeled and grated
1 medium onion, finely chopped
2 tablespoons cilantro leaves, chopped
½ teaspoon salt
½ teaspoon ground turmeric
2–3 green chiles, finely chopped
2 cups oil, for deep frying

1 Wash the lentils and place in a bowl. Cover with hot water and leave to soak for 30 minutes. Drain and place in a food processor or blender with the grated ginger. Blend to form a thick paste. Pour into a mixing bowl.

2 Stir in the onion, cilantro leaves, salt, turmeric, and chiles, and mix thoroughly. Shape spoonfuls of the mixture into balls.

3 Meanwhile, heat the oil in a deep fryer to 375°F, or half-fill a saucepan with oil and heat to 375°F or until a cube of bread dropped into it sizzles fairly vigorously. Fry the piaju, in batches, for about 1 minute or until golden brown. Lift out of the oil using a slotted spoon, and place on a plate lined with paper towels to absorb any excess oil. Serve hot with lemon wedges and Raita (see below).

Raita (Indian yogurt sauce)

½ cucumber
1 cup plain yogurt
1–2 garlic cloves, crushed
10 fresh mint leaves, shredded
salt and freshly ground black pepper

Prepare 10 minutes | **Serves** 6

1 Cut the cucumber in half lengthwise, scoop out the seeds with a teaspoon and discard them. Finely chop the flesh and pat dry with paper towels. Put the yogurt in a bowl and stir in the garlic and shredded mint.

2 Season to taste, then spoon into a smaller serving dish to serve.

"In a society where the rights and potential of women are constrained, no man can be truly free. He may have power, but he will not have freedom."

Mary Robinson

Leek and potato soup

2 tablespoons olive oil
2–3 leeks, about 8oz, finely chopped
4 cups vegetable stock
2 potatoes, about 14oz, diced
½ teaspoon caraway seeds (optional)
heavy cream, to serve (optional)
salt and freshly ground black pepper

This was my father-in-law's favorite soup, and it is popular throughout Ireland, where we have the good fortune to grow excellent potatoes. It always amazes me how this humble dish packs such power!

Prepare 5 minutes | **Cook** 35 minutes | **Serves** 4

1 Heat the oil in a large pan or flameproof casserole over medium heat and gently cook the leeks with a splash of the vegetable stock for 5 minutes, or until translucent.

2 Pour in the remaining vegetable stock and bring to a boil. Add the potatoes and caraway seeds (if using) and season.

3 Simmer for 25–30 minutes, or until the potato is tender. Pour into a blender or food processor and blend until smooth. Taste and adjust the seasoning, then allow to cool for 3–4 minutes before serving. Serve with a swirl of cream, if liked.

Cook's tip

Serve this soup with the soda bread on page 137 for a delicious, hearty meal.

Cheese soufflé

4 tablespoons butter, plus extra
for greasing
³/₄ oz Parmesan cheese, grated
plus extra for dusting
¹/₄ cup all-purpose flour
³/₄ cup milk
3¹/₂ oz Cheddar cheese, or other
hard cheese (I throw in old bits of
hard cheese), grated
2 tablespoons tomato paste
1 tablespoon Dijon mustard
pinch of cayenne
pepper (optional)
3 egg yolks
5 egg whites
salt and freshly ground
black pepper

Prepare 15 minutes | **Cook** 25–30 minutes, depending on dish | **Serves** 4

1 Preheat the oven to 375°F. Grease 4 × 8¹/₂ oz soufflé dishes or 1 1-quart dish with butter and line with half of the grated Parmesan cheese. Melt the butter in a saucepan over medium heat. Stir in the flour and cook for 1 minute. Remove from the heat and gradually stir in the milk, then return to the heat, stirring constantly, until the sauce comes to the boil. Cook, stirring, for about 1 minute. Remove from the heat and stir in the Cheddar and remaining Parmesan cheese until melted. Mix in the tomato paste, mustard and cayenne pepper (if using). Beat in the egg yolks, season to taste and set aside.

2 In a clean bowl, whisk the egg whites with a pinch of salt until stiff (but not dry) peaks form. To test whether the egg whites are ready, you can turn the dish on its side and the whites should hold their shape.

3 Stir a quarter of the egg white mixture into the cheese sauce. Then gently and carefully fold in the remaining egg whites, trying not to lose too much of the air.

4 Carefully spoon the mixture into the prepared dish or dishes, sprinkle with Parmesan and arrange on a baking sheet. Cook in the oven for about 10–15 minutes for the smaller soufflés or 30–35 minutes for the larger one, until well risen and golden in color. Don't keep opening the oven or they will deflate. Serve immediately.

"I am not bitter. I am hopeful for myself, my community, and my country."
Elizabeth, WfWI Rwanda participant

Emma Bridgewater and Matthew Rice: Cheese and leek tart

For the dough
1²/₃ cups all-purpose flour
pinch of salt
1 stick butter, chilled and cut into cubes, plus extra for greasing

For the filling
2 tablespoons butter
4 leeks, washed and sliced
3 large eggs
1 cup light cream
2 tablespoons of your favorite mustard
1 ³/₄ cups Cheddar or goat cheese, grated

For the salad
7oz mixed green leaves
1 tablespoon chopped parsley

For the dressing
4 tablespoons olive oil
2 teaspoons white wine vinegar
2 teaspoons brown sugar
squeeze of lemon juice
salt and freshly ground black pepper

Prepare 25 minutes, plus 30 minutes resting | **Cook** 1 hour 10 minutes | **Serves** 4

1 First, make the dough. Place the flour in a large mixing bowl with the salt and add the butter. Rub the butter into the flour using your fingertips until it resembles fine bread crumbs. Then sprinkle 1½ tablespoons cold water into the rubbed-in mixture, and mix with a round-bladed knife until a dough starts to form. Draw the mixture together with your hands until it makes a rough ball. If the mixture is too dry and will not form a ball, add a few extra drops of water. Take care not to make the dough sticky—it will be difficult to handle and produce tough dough. Wrap the dough in plastic wrap and refrigerate for at least 30 minutes.

2 Preheat the oven to 350°F, and grease a 10-inch round tart pan (ideally with a loose bottom). Roll out the chilled dough on a lightly floured work surface, until big enough for the pan, and line the prepared pan with the rolled out dough. Use the prongs of a fork to prick all over, then line the dough with a piece of parchment paper paper and fill with uncooked rice, dried beans, or baking beans before placing in the oven. Bake blind for 25–30 minutes, remove from the oven, and discard the parchment paper and baking beans. Return the pie crust to the oven for another 10 minutes, until the dough is just cooked but not colored, then remove it from the oven and allow to cool.

3 Meanwhile, make the filling. Melt the butter in a frying pan and gently cook the leeks for 10–15 minutes, until soft. In a bowl, beat the eggs with the cream and mustard, then stir in the grated cheese. Season and pour this mixture into the pie crust, then bake in the oven for 25–30 minutes, or until the filling has just set.

4 While the tart is cooking, make the dressing for the salad. Combine the olive oil and white wine vinegar with the brown sugar and a squeeze of lemon juice, as well as a pinch of sea salt and a grind of black pepper. Mix the leaves with the chopped parsley and toss with the dressing. Serve with the warm tart.

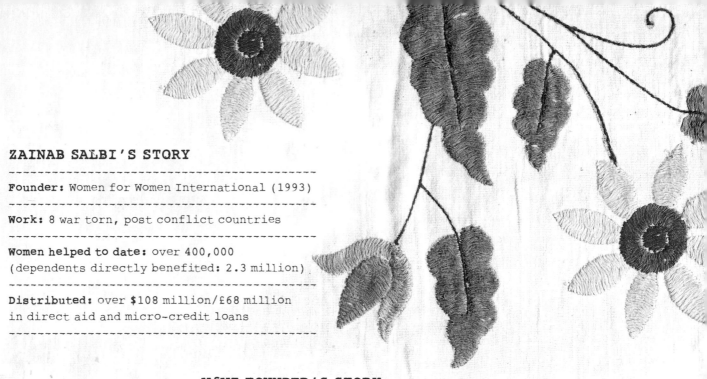

ZAINAB SALBI'S STORY

Founder: Women for Women International (1993)

Work: 8 war torn, post conflict countries

Women helped to date: over 400,000
(dependents directly benefited: 2.3 million)

Distributed: over $108 million/£68 million
in direct aid and micro-credit loans

WfWI FOUNDER'S STORY
----

*"The reason and spirit behind Women for Women International
is to understand war from a woman's perspective. I felt the need to
acknowledge women affected by war; to support them in the process
of rebuilding their lives and to create a safe space for them
to tell their stories and build their community."*

Zainab Salbi

We each have a choice to make in this life: to live life out of fear or to live life out of love. In both cases, we each live our lives in the hope of fulfilling our full potential as the route to joy and happiness. Sometimes we are conscious of our journey and sometimes we are not. In my case, it took me years to be conscious that in founding Women for Women International, I was seeking my truth as I sought every woman's truth. I broke my own silence as I heard women survivors of war break their own silence. I was finding my own rhythm for the larger dance that we are all part of as I witnessed the beats of women in Rwanda, Bosnia and Iraq, among others.

What started as a journey against the injustice that women in wartime face ended up being a journey of love and joy in the process of witnessing women rebuild their lives one step at a time, starting with hope, then learning about the possibilities of change through awareness, then learning to make something tangible, then earning a living and speaking up. I am not proud of anything. I am just grateful for the journey and all the women and men that I encountered in the process. Through serving and witnessing women finding their peace, I was able to also find mine and for that, I am just very grateful.

Celebration recipes - Zainab Salbi

I am the kind of cook who is constantly inventing and revising. I could never follow a recipe, but constantly make new recipes for myself. I just open the refrigerator, see what inspires me, and go from there to make something new. The look of a dish is as important as its taste for me. My mother used to always tell me, "The eyes eat before the mouth," and I follow this rule religiously. These salads are my inventions and both have the memory of cooking in a camp that I go to every year where there is no electricity or running water. It is a complete immersion in nature and, as there is no stove, most meals comprise salad and grills. It is my favorite time of the year and it is when all my cooking creativity comes through as I make the salads in the wilderness, surrounded by beautiful lakes and the quietness of nature. May these dishes bring you the joy that they have brought me.

Beet salad

This salad is full of surprises, from the raw beets to the fresh ginger. It's colorful, beautiful and very healthy.

Prepare 20 minutes | **Serves** 6 as a side dish

4 beets
2 carrots
2 celery ribs
1 avocado
1-inch piece fresh ginger, peeled and finely chopped
1 tablespoon sesame seeds
1 tablespoon fresh cilantro, chopped
6 tablespoons olive oil
2 tablespoons balsamic vinegar
salt and freshly ground black pepper

1 Peel the beets and carrots and cut these and the celery into small, even cubes. Place in a salad bowl.
2 Peel and pit the avocado and cut the flesh into cubes. Add to the bowl and gently mix to combine.
3 Add the ginger, sesame seeds, and cilantro. Pour in the olive oil and balsamic vinegar. Season, gently mix, and serve.

Celery salad

Prepare 10 minutes | **Serves** 2-4 as side

4 celery ribs
1/2 cup walnuts
2 peaches
2/3 cup (4oz) feta cheese, cubed
2 tablespoons finely chopped fresh cilantro
2 tablespoons olive oil
1-2 tablespoons lemon juice, or to taste
salt and freshly ground black pepper

1 Thinly slice the celery and roughly chop the walnuts, and place in a serving bowl. Peel and pit the peaches and cut the flesh into cubes. Add to the serving bowl.
2 Add the feta and cilantro. Gently mix together, then drizzle with the olive oil and lemon juice. Season and serve.

"When I visited Rwanda with Women for Women International in 2010, the highlight of the trip was talking with girls and women who were being trained as national organic farming extension agents. What an inspiration it was to see women transforming not only themselves but also the landscape, families and society in this way!"

Jennifer Buffett

Kale salad

1 lb kale
juice of ½ lemon
1 cup extra virgin olive oil
5 tablespoons balsamic vinegar
1–2 garlic cloves, crushed
1 egg, beaten
³/₄ cup Parmesan or
Grana Padano cheese, grated
½ cup salted hazelnuts, chopped
½ cup dried currants

Kale keeps for longer than lettuce so you can prepare this salad and store it overnight in an airtight container in the refrigerator. It tastes even better the next day.

Prepare 10 minutes | **Serves** 4–6

1 Using your hands, gently tear the kale leaves away from the coarse center stalks and discard the stalks. Tear the kale leaves into smaller bite-size pieces and place in a large salad bowl.

2 Squeeze in the lemon juice and mix into the kale. In a small bowl, make a dressing by whisking together the olive oil, balsamic vinegar, and garlic, then stir in the egg. Season, then pour the dressing over the kale and, using your hand, toss through the kale evenly.

3 Add the grated cheese, nuts, and currants and gently stir to combine.

Potato salad

2 lbs small new or baby potatoes
1 tablespoon wholegrain mustard
²/₃ cup sour cream
1 red onion, finely chopped
2 tablespoons fresh chives, finely
chopped
2 tablespoons fresh dill, torn
¹/₃ cup pickles or
cornichons, chopped
4 hardboiled eggs, peeled
2 containers cress
salt and freshly
ground black pepper

Prepare 15 minutes | **Cook** 15 minutes | **Serves** 8

1 Fill a large pan with water. Place over medium heat, add the potatoes and salt to taste, and bring to a boil. Cook for 10–15 minutes or until tender, drain, and set aside to cool completely.

2 Slice the cooled potatoes and place in a large bowl. Stir the mustard into the sour cream and season. Pour into the bowl, add the red onion, herbs, and chopped pickles or cornichons and gently toss to combine. Quarter the eggs and add to the salad. Top with snipped cress.

Top, Kale salad. **Bottom left**, Potato salad.
Bottom right, Orange, watercress, and pumpkin seed salad (page 205)

"The great gift of human beings is that we have the power of empathy."
Meryl Streep

Wheatberry salad

²/₃ cup wheat berries

4–6 pepperoncini, or pickled green peppers

4–5 scallions green parts only, sliced,

2 tablespoons extra virgin olive oil

2 tablespoons mint leaves, chopped

²/₃ cup pomegranate seeds

²/₃ cup feta cheese, cubed

I have approximated this recipe from a salad I enjoyed at the Grocer On Elgin in London. This was my lunch of choice every single day we shot the film *Mamma Mia*, in the rainiest summer London had seen for a while. It evoked Greece, and smiles, and has a bright, light taste. Enjoy!

Prepare 10 minutes | **Cook** 45 minutes | **Serves** 4–6 as a side dish

1 Cook the wheat berries according to the package instructions. Set aside to cool completely, then transfer into a bowl.

2 Add the pepperoncini or pickled green peppers, scallions, and olive oil and toss to combine.

3 Stir in the mint and pomegranate seeds and toss in the cheese. Season to taste. This salad is great served at room temperature or chilled.

Orange, watercress, and pumpkin seed salad
(pictured page 203)

7oz watercress

2 oranges or pink grapefruits, peeled and cut into segments, juice reserved

2 ripe avocados, peeled, stoned and cut into chunks

2 tablespoons canola oil

2 teaspoons Dijon mustard

1 teaspoon sugar

³/₄ cup pumpkin seeds, toasted

salt and freshly ground black pepper

Prepare 10 minutes | **Serves** 8

1 Place the watercress in a bowl with the orange or grapefruit segments and the avocado.

2 Whisk the oil with the mustard, sugar, and 1 tablespoon of the reserved orange or grapefruit juice, and season. Dress the salad with the citrus dressing, scatter with the toasted seeds, and serve.

"The letters I received from my sponsor warmed my heart. A woman who had never seen or met me had put her faith in me and made a commitment to change my life. If she was so committed to helping me improve my life, why should I not do it for myself?"

Nazmije, WfWI Kosovo participant

Yotam Ottolenghi: Castelluccio lentils with tomatoes and Gorgonzola

1 small red onion, very thinly sliced
1 tablespoon good quality red wine vinegar
1 teaspoon sea salt
1 cup Castelluccio lentils
3 tablespoons olive oil
1 garlic clove, crushed
3 tablespoons chopped chervil (or parsley)
3 tablespoons chopped chives
3 tablespoons chopped dill
2³/₄ oz mild Gorgonzola, cut into rough chunks
salt and freshly ground black pepper
For the oven-dried tomatoes
14 oz plum tomatoes (about 5)
8 thyme sprigs
1 tablespoon olive oil
2 tablespoons thick balsamic vinegar

My obsessive relationship with food started off very one-sided: I enjoyed eating and I enjoyed it immensely. It was only later on in life I learned the joy of feeding, the sheer pleasure of witnessing someone relishing something I created. I am incredibly fortunate to now have both. Italian-inspired, this recipe has everything I want from a substantial salad: delicate jewel-like lentils, robust oven tomatoes, fresh green herbs and the requisite amount of decadence from the creamy cheese.

Prepare 10 minutes | **Cook** 1½ hours | **Serves** 4

1 Start by making the oven-dried tomatoes. Preheat the oven to 250°F. Quarter the tomatoes vertically and place skin-side down on a baking sheet lined with parchment paper. Arrange the thyme sprigs on top of them. Drizzle over the olive oil and balsamic vinegar and sprinkle with some salt. Roast for 1½ hours or until semi-dried. Discard the thyme and allow to cool down slightly.

2 Meanwhile, place the red onion in a medium bowl, pour over the vinegar and sprinkle with the sea salt. Stir, then leave for a few minutes so the onion softens a bit.

3 Place the lentils in a pan of boiling water (the water should come 1¹/₄ inches above the lentils) and cook for 20–30 minutes or until tender. Drain well in a sieve and, while still warm, add to the sliced onion. Also add the olive oil, garlic and some black pepper. Stir to mix and leave aside to cool down. Once cool, add the herbs and gently mix together. Taste and adjust the seasoning.

4 To serve, pile up the lentils on a large plate or bowl, integrating the Gorgonzola and tomatoes as you build up the pile. Drizzle the tomato cooking juices on top and serve.

"I learned that courage was not the absence of fear, but the triumph over it. I felt fear myself more times than I can remember, but I hid it behind a mask of boldness. The brave man is not he who does not feel afraid, but he who conquers that fear."

Nelson Mandela

Caranguejo recheado (stuffed crab)

5 lbs small crabs, cleaned and steamed

4 slices white bread

1–2 tablespoons of milk (or enough to soak the bread)

2 medium onions, finely chopped

2 tablespoons olive oil

2 garlic cloves, crushed

2 large red chiles (melegueta), finely chopped

1 bay leaf

1 tablespoon lemon juice

2 tablespoons grated Parmesan cheese

1 egg, separated

1 tablespoon finely chopped parsley

This recipe, one of Nelson Mandela's favourites, was created for him by his chef in Maputo, Esmenia Rafael Gemo.

Prepare 15 minutes | **Cook** 20 minutes | **Serves** 4

1 Preheat the oven to 300°F. Take the crab meat from inside the shells and cut it into small pieces. Retain the crab shells, because you are going to stuff them.

2 Soak the bread in the milk.

3 In a pan, sauté the onions over low heat in the olive oil until soft, and then add the garlic, chiles and bay leaf. Increase the heat, and add the crab meat and lemon juice and mix well. Remove the bread from the milk and add it to the crab mixture. Once everything is well combined, add the grated cheese and remove the mixture from the heat. Transfer the mixture to a bowl, and let it cool. When the mixture is cool, add the egg white and the chopped parsley.

4 Put the crab mixture into the reserved crab shells and brush with the egg yolk. Place the stuffed crabs in the oven for 15 minutes. Serve hot.

"The education and empowerment of women throughout the world cannot fail to result in a more caring, tolerant, just and peaceful life for all."

Aung San Suu Kyi

Burmese tomato fish curry

10oz firm, sustainable white fish, cut into cubes

10oz raw peeled shrimp

2 teaspoons ground turmeric

2 tablespoons fish sauce

5 shallots

2–3 red chiles (deseeded if you prefer)

5 garlic cloves

1 inch piece fresh ginger, peeled

3 tablespoons vegetable oil

½ teaspoon paprika

28 oz fresh tomatoes, chopped

1 cup fish or vegetable stock

2 tablespoons fresh cilantro

1 lime, cut into wedges, to serve

A classic fish curry made that is quick to make, with chunks of fish and shrimp in a warming fragrant tomato sauce.

Prepare 10 minutes, plus 10 minutes marinating | **Cook** 20 minutes | **Serves** 4

1 Mix together the turmeric, fish sauce and a splash of water to make a paste. Coat the fish and shrimp with it, and set aside on a plate for 15–20 minutes to marinate.

2 Meanwhile place the shallots, chillies, garlic and ginger in a food processor or blender and blitz together until they form a paste. Heat the oil in a deep frying or sauté pan and fry the paste for 2–3 minutes until softened and fragrant smelling. Add the paprika and cook for a further minute.

3 Add the chopped tomatoes and fry for 5–6 minutes until they are softened. Pour in the stock and bring to the boil. Stir in the shrimp and cook for 2 minutes, then stir in the fish. Cover and leave to simmer gently for about 5 minutes, or until the shrimp are pink and opaque and the fish is just cooked.

4 Reserve some of the cilantro for garnish and coarsely chop the rest. Gently stir into the curry and season to taste with extra fish sauce and lime juice. Serve with steamed rice, garnished with the reserved cilantro.

A SPONSOR'S STORY

- -

*"Taking care of our local and global selves—our people, our soil,
our waters, our air—and providing opportunity for the healthiest options
for everyone—rich and in need—is humanly respectful."*

Jesse Ziff Cool

I have been reading about life in Africa for years. The hardship of women and
children, in the midst of the worst darkness, reaches me most deeply. The stories
became a sort of spiritual experience, opening wide the world outside my usual
way of thinking. No matter how impossible the gut-wrenching accounts are to accept,
sometimes, in the midst of the worst despair and at the end of an unspeakable
situation, there is the purest sense of forgiveness, love and hope.

Through Women for Women International I sponsored a woman named Odette who lives
in Rwanda. I travelled to Rwanda to learn more about the organization. It was also
an opportunity to actualize my reading. My hope was to open doors by finding a way
to farm and cook with the women there and, of course, to meet Odette.

I packed 18 pairs of cooking tongs and lots of organic seed packets. The word spread
quickly through my interpreter, Assumpta, that in the US I grow food and am a cook.
Heart-warming connections unfolded while weeding, peeling vegetables, cooking over
open fires and sitting at tables sharing stories with my new women friends.

To meet Odette and her family, we walked down steep mountain trails to her home.
Waiting for us was a meal prepared from her garden of boiled potatoes, beans and
green bananas smothered in groundnut sauce. I have eaten amazing food, but this
was one of the most memorable meals of my life.

Memories of the genocide in Rwanda remain. My reading helped me to prepare for this
part of the trip. But it was in the kitchens, where we stirred up aromatic spoonfuls
of deliciousness, that I discovered that love and kindness prevail over all.

Celebration recipes – Jesse Ziff Cool

Staying connected to where our food comes from and the people who produce it is at the core of a healthy community. Making sure the people element of sustainability is number one ensures well-being for everyone.

Slow-cooked pork with potatoes and greens

I love the universality of this recipe. It can be cooked in a slow cooker or over an open fire in a deep, heavy pot. Any cut of beef or goat that is suitable for slow cooking can be substituted for the pork. And instead of potatoes, consider any root vegetable such as beets, rutabaga, or yams. In place of hearty greens add spinach, or a more delicate wild green like dandelions during the last 15 minutes of cooking. Adjust the flavoring or add hot chiles to make the dish even more exciting.

Prepare 15 minutes, plus 30 minutes standing | **Cook** 3 hours 45 minutes | **Serves** 6-8

5 lb pork shoulder
2 tablespoons chopped garlic
1½ teaspoons ground cumin (optional)
4 tablespoons white or red wine vinegar
2 tablespoons muscovado, palm, or brown sugar
2-3 medium potatoes, peeled
1 lb baby leaf greens, such as chard, escarole, or kale, coarsely chopped
salt and freshly ground black pepper

1 Place the pork in a lidded, deep baking pan and add the garlic, cumin, vinegar, sugar, and seasoning. Rub all over the meat to coat thoroughly. Cover and set aside to stand at room temperature for 30 minutes.
2 Preheat the oven to 450° F. Roast the pork for 30 minutes, then reduce the heat to 300° F and continue cooking, uncovered, for 2-2½ hours, basting occasionally with the pan juices.
3 Slice the potatoes and greens into large bite-size pieces and add them to the pan,

tossing to coat in the juices. Cover the pot, return to the oven and cook for another 45 minutes or until the pork and potatoes are tender.
4 Transfer the pork to a cutting board. Spoon the vegetables and juices onto a serving platter. Slice or pull the pork apart with a fork, put on top of the vegetables and serve.

Cabbage and pepper slaw with ginger

I make this salad frequently and enjoy it on its own or with pork, chicken or tofu.

Prepare 15 minutes, plus 1 hour standing time | **Serves** 6-8

1 small red cabbage, about 1 lb, thinly sliced
1 small white cabbage, about 1 lb, thinly sliced
½ red pepper, deseeded and thinly sliced
½ red onion, thinly sliced
2 tablespoons cilantro leaves, chopped
1-inch piece fresh ginger, peeled and finely chopped
¼-½ teaspoon red pepper flakes, to taste
½ cup rice wine vinegar
2 tablespoons olive oil
pinch of sugar
salt and freshly ground black pepper

1 Combine all of the ingredients in a large bowl and season to taste. Cover and refrigerate for at least an hour, preferably longer or overnight.
2 Adjust the seasoning to taste and serve.

"seasonal produce, picked at its peak of ripeness, is the basis of everything I do. My aim is to make superior produce available to everyone, regardless of cooking skills. I hope I can share my love of good food with you all."

Maggie Beer

Chicken with vino cotto

8 chicken drumsticks
zest and juice of 2 lemons
5 fresh bay leaves
2 stalks rosemary
½ teaspoon ground cinnamon
2 tablespoons extra virgin
olive oil
½ cup sliced almonds
3 tablespoons unsalted butter
4 tablespoons vino cotto
or balsamic vinegar
16 green olives, pitted
½ cup raisins
⅓ cup salted capers, rinsed
and drained
chopped fresh flat-leaf
parsley, to serve
salt

My daughter Saskia raises chickens, so I often turn to chicken when looking for something to cook for a crowd. I find that chicken drumsticks are well suited because no carving is required, and this dish has the added benefit of being served straight from the cooking pot. It's also fantastic eaten cold the next day, when the pan juices have become jellied. Sometimes I use caperberries instead of capers, but they can be a bit vinegary, so use less and soak in cold water first.

Prepare 20 minutes, plus 1 hour marinating | **Cook** 35 minutes | **Serves** 4

1 Place the chicken in a dish with the lemon zest, bay leaves, rosemary, cinnamon, and olive oil and leave to marinate for at least 1 hour before cooking (overnight is even better, if you have time).

2 Preheat the oven to 400°F. Sprinkle the almonds onto a baking sheet and roast for 5 minutes or until golden, then set aside to cool. Increase the oven temperature to 425°F.

3 Heat the butter in a large ovenproof frying pan over medium heat. Season the chicken with salt, then remove it from the marinade. Working in batches so you don't overcrowd the pan, gently cook the chicken for 8–10 minutes, or until golden brown all over, turning once. Transfer the pan to the oven and roast for 10 minutes. Drain off any excess fat.

4 Place the pan over high heat and add the vino cotto or balsamic vinegar to deglaze, then add the olives, raisins, and capers. Return to the oven for 10 minutes, or until the chicken is thoroughly cooked through.

5 Sprinkle the almonds and parsley over the chicken, then squeeze over the lemon juice to taste. Allow to rest for 10 minutes before serving.

> *"Only when old politicians start bumping into new politicians, who have been specifically elected to represent the health of the planet, and who now threaten the cozy status quo, will they start getting the point. This stuff matters, and it's time to do something about it."*
>
> **Hugh Fearnley-Whittingstall**

Sticky glazed spare ribs

3 lb 5oz pork ribs
(roughly 2 whole racks' worth)

For the marinade
6 tablespoons currant,
plum, apple, or other fruit jelly
2 tablespoons honey
2 garlic cloves, crushed to a paste
1 tablespoon finely grated
fresh ginger
½ –1 medium-hot red chile,
finely chopped, or ½ teaspoon
dried red pepper flakes
2 tablespoons soy sauce

For the roast squash
1 large butternut squash,
around 2 lbs, or the equivalent
weight of acorn
or other squash or pumpkin
6–8 fat garlic cloves, skin on,
lightly squashed
a few sprigs of rosemary
1 fairly hot red chile, seeded
and finely chopped
4–5 tablespoons canola
or olive oil, plus extra to serve
¼ cup pine nuts or walnuts
(optional)
Juice of ½ lemon
Sea salt and freshly ground
black pepper

These sweet, sticky, spicy ribs make an excellent dish to share with friends—no one can stand on ceremony while tucking into them. Make sure you keep a few back for a solitary treat to be nibbled cold once everyone has gone home. You can roast the ribs as whole racks, which looks great, or to make serving easier, ask the butcher to chop them into one- or two-rib pieces.

Prepare 10 minutes, plus 1 hour marinating | **Cook** 1½ hours | **Serves** 6–8

1 Combine all the marinade ingredients, whisking them together well. Put the ribs in a large baking dish, pour the marinade over them, and use your hands or a brush to get them well coated. Cover and leave to marinate in a cool place for at least an hour, or for several hours in the fridge, turning them from time to time.
2 Preheat the oven to 325°F. Turn the ribs in their marinade, cover the dish with foil, and bake for 45 minutes.
3 Increase the oven temperature to 375°F. Remove the foil and turn the ribs again, basting them with the sauce. Cook the ribs, uncovered, for 35–45 minutes, turning and basting them 2 or 3 more times, until they are glossy and dark and coated in the caramelized sauce.
4 Remove from the oven and spoon any remaining sauce from the dish over the ribs. Leave until they are cool enough to pick up with your fingers, then tuck in. Serve with steamed rice and wilted greens, or with a side serving of roast squash (see below).

Roast squash with chile, garlic, and rosemary

Prepare 10 minutes | **Cook** 55 minutes | **Serves** 4

1 Preheat the oven to 375°F. Slice the squash into quarters and seed it, scooping out the seeds with a spoon. I leave the skin on most squashes when I'm roasting them, but you can peel it off if you prefer. Cut the squash into wedges or chunks and put them in a small roasting pan.
2 Add the garlic and rosemary, the chopped chile and lots of salt and pepper. Trickle over 2–3 tablespoons of the oil and toss together.
3 Roast in the oven for 40–55 minutes, stirring halfway through, until the squash is completely soft and starting to caramelize.
4 Meanwhile, if using nuts, toast them in a dry frying pan over medium heat for a few minutes, until golden brown, then scatter them over the roasted squash. Add a squeeze of lemon juice and another good trickle of oil, then serve.

*"I'm an okay cook. I'm an okay businesswoman.
I am, however, a terrific Picker of People. People who are passionate
about what they do and want to do it properly.
There is nothing better, and then they can achieve miracles.
It's just about having the right attitude."*

Prue Leith

Teriyaki roast lamb

2 ¹/₂ lb leg of lamb, boned
²/₃ cup teriyaki sauce
2 tablespoons honey
1 tablespoon oil

This is perfect celebration dinner party food. Just put it in the oven when you hear the doorbell. After half an hour take it out, and start on the first course while the lamb rests. No need to make gravy either, the juices and the teriyaki do that.

Prepare 10 minutes, plus at least 30 minutes marinating
| **Cook** 25 minutes | **Serves** 4

1 Ask your butcher to bone the lamb for you, opening it out flat, or butterfly the lamb so that it is flat and of a uniform thickness.
2 Place the lamb in a nonmetallic dish. Pour in the teriyaki sauce and honey, cover, and refrigerate. Allow to marinate for up to 24 hours, turning occasionally. (If you forget, don't worry. It's nice with only 30 minutes marinating, too.)
3 Preheat the oven to 450°F. Lay the lamb skin-side up in an oiled roasting pan. Cover with the marinade. Roast for 25–30 minutes, and then leave to stand for 20 minutes before slicing and serving.

"Appreciate life, respect others, and learn from failures. And never forget where you came from."

Michelle Sampoerna

Indonesian beef rendang

3 tablespoons vegetable oil

2 lbs stewing or shin of beef, cut into 1-inch cubes

14oz can coconut milk

1 cup beef stock

For the spice paste

10 red chiles, seeded

10 shallots, peeled

5 garlic cloves

1-inch piece fresh ginger, peeled

1–2 teaspoons ground turmeric

1-inch piece fresh galangal, peeled, or 2 teaspoons galangal paste

1 teaspoon ground nutmeg

½ tablespoon coriander seeds

For the whole spices

3 kaffir lime leaves

3 bay leaves

1 stalk lemongrass, crushed

2 cardamom pods

½ cinnamon stick

To garnish

cilantro leaves

lime wedges

This delicious, spicy dish is traditionally prepared in Indonesian communities for festive occasions and to honor guests. It takes a long time to cook but the end result, fragrant and warming, is well worth it.

Prepare 20 minutes | **Cook** 3 hours 10 minutes | **Serves** 4–6

1 Preheat the oven to 300°F. Place all of the spices for the spice paste into a small blender or food processor and blend to form a smooth paste (or use a mortar and pestle).

2 Heat the oil in a large lidded pan over medium heat and fry the spice paste for 4–5 minutes, or until fragrant. Add the beef and all of the whole spices and cook for another 5 minutes, or until the meat is browned.

3 Pour in the coconut milk and stock, then cover. Place in the oven for 2½–3 hours, or until the beef is tender. Remove the whole spices, if visible. Serve garnished with fresh cilantro leaves and wedges of lime and accompanied by steamed rice.

"When we all invest in girls, everyone wins: girls, their families, their communities and their nations. We call this the girl effect."

Maria Eitel

Kleftiko (Greek roast lamb)

3 onions, thickly sliced

2 garlic heads, quartered horizontally

²⁄₃ cup dry white wine

2 tablespoons olive oil

3 tablespoons fresh oregano leaves

4 ½–5 ½ lb leg of lamb

1 ¹⁄₃ lbs small new or baby potatoes, scrubbed

1 lemon, sliced

salt and freshly ground black pepper

For the yogurt sauce

2 teaspoon coriander seeds

1 teaspoon cumin seeds

juice of ½ lemon

2 tablespoons extra virgin olive oil

2 tablespoons roughly chopped mint

1 ¹⁄₄ cups plain yogurt

This traditional Greek lemon and garlic infused lamb is cooked for 5 hours, resulting in deliciously tender meat packed with flavor.

Prepare 25 minutes | **Cook** 5 hours | **Serves** 6

1 Preheat the oven to 350°F. Line a large roasting pan with foil, covering the sides and base. Line the foil with parchment paper. Arrange the onions in the roasting pan and top with one of the quartered garlic heads. Pour in the white wine.

2 Mix the oil with the oregano and season, then rub well into the lamb. Place the lamb in the roasting pan on top of the onions. Cover with parchment paper and foil, sealing the ends well. Place in the oven and cook for 3 hours.

3 Open the foil and parchment paper. Add the potatoes, stir into the juices, then add the sliced lemon and remaining garlic. Stir once more until well coated. Re-cover tightly and return to the oven for another 2 hours.

4 Meanwhile, make the yogurt sauce. Toast the coriander and cumin seeds, then lightly crush with a mortar and pestle. Mix with the lemon juice, olive oil, and mint. Stir into the yogurt and season to taste. Cover and chill until ready to serve.

5 Transfer the lamb to a large platter or board, cover, and keep warm while the meat rests. Meanwhile, spoon the potatoes and lemon into a bowl, then pour the lamb juices and onions into a seperate bowl. Serve these with the lamb, the yogurt sauce and a big green salad or wilted greens.

Talia Leman: Best-ever challah

1¼ teaspoons yeast

1 large egg, beaten, plus 1 egg
to glaze

⅓ cup sugar

2 teaspoons kosher or sea salt

⅓–½ cup canola oil

4–5½ cups bread flour, plus
extra for flouring

For the filling (optional)

1 x can Solo Poppy Seed Filling

⅛–¼ cup honey

½ cup chopped nuts (I prefer
pecan or walnut)

To finish (optional)

poppy seeds or turbinado sugar

Optional filling

1 Pour the poppy seed filling, honey and nuts into a bowl and mix until you have a spreadable paste.

2 Distribute scoops of the filling along each dough rectangle, and coat the dough thinly and evenly using your hands, back of a spoon or a spatula. Leave ½ an inch of uncovered dough (no filling) all the way around the edge.

3 Roll up the dough rectangles along the long edge, and pinch together one of the ends tightly. Now resume with step 6.

This recipe was created by my mother, Dana Mintzer Leman, who worked her way through countless challah recipes in order to perfect this one for our family. After years of honing, it has arrived at the point where everyone who tastes it exclaims, "This is the best challah ever!" Trust me, it is, and it also makes the best French toast ever, too.

Prepare 15 minutes, plus rising | **Cook** 35–40 minutes | **Makes** 1 large loaf

1 Put the yeast into the bowl of an electric mixer fitted with the dough attachment. Pour in 1½ cups warm water and proof the yeast by sprinkling a little sugar over the water and seeing if it bubbles after 5–10 minutes. Add the egg, sugar, salt and 5 tablespoons of the oil. Mix to combine, then fold in 4 cups of the flour using a spatula. Start the mixer and add the remaining flour, a little at a time, until it forms a smooth ball. (I stir each addition with a spatula before turning the mixer back on so the flour doesn't fly everywhere.) You will know you have added the perfect amount of flour when your thumb sticks to the dough for just a second before coming away clean. On humid days you may need to add more flour, but don't add too much.

2 To prepare the oven, turn it on to warm for 60 seconds and then turn it off. Place a pan of boiling water in the oven, to create steam.

3 Pour the remaining oil over the dough and turn to coat. Partially cover the bowl with plastic wrap, leaving a gap to allow the steam to reach the dough. Place in the oven and let rise for 2 hours.

4 Turn the dough out onto a lightly floured surface. Punch the dough down and knead lightly. Return to the bowl and repeat stages 2 and 3.

5 Now you are ready to form the challah. Again turn the dough out onto a lightly floured surface. The dough should not be sticky and should form a soft, smooth and well-formed ball. Divide the dough into 3 or 6 equal-sized pieces. If you are not adding filling, shape them into long logs, about 12 inches long . If you are including the filling, shape them into rectangles about 2–3 times as long as they are wide and add the filling according to the instructions (see left).

6 Braid the dough together to form the challah. Transfer onto a baking sheet lined with non-stick parchment paper, and leave in a warm place to rise for an hour.

7 Preheat the oven to 375°F. Whisk the egg with 1 tablespoon water and brush over the risen challah, then scatter with the poppy seeds or turbinado sugar, if using. Bake for 35–40 minutes or so until the bread is browned and has a hollow sound when tapped on the bottom. You can tell it's ready when the parts of the challah that are exposed between the braids look mildly toasted.

8 Transfer to a cooling rack and leave to cool for at least 20 minutes, uncovered (otherwise the bread will sweat and get soggy) before serving.

"Because I can. That is the single best reason to do anything."
Talia Leman

"Every human being is precious. Do your little bit of good where you are. It's those little bits of good put together that overwhelm the world."

Archbishop Desmond Tutu

Exotic fruit salad with passion fruit syrup

¹/₄ cup sugar

4 passion fruits

1 large pineapple

juice of 1 lemon

1 ripe mango, peeled, pitted, and diced

2 ripe papayas, peeled, seeded, and cut into chunks

12 lychees, peeled

4 sprigs fresh mint

2 bananas

1 lime, cut into wedges, and

single cream, to serve

Refreshing and perfect for serving on hot summer days. Vary the fruit according to what is in season.

Prepare 15 minutes | **Cook** 10 minutes | **Serves** 6

1 Place the sugar in a small pan over low heat. Pour in ½ cup cold water and heat gently for 2–3 minutes, or until the sugar dissolves. Increase the heat to medium, bring to a simmer, and cook for 5 minutes, or until the mixture forms a thin syrup. Set aside to cool.

2 Cut the passion fruit in half, scoop out the flesh and seeds, and stir into the cooled syrup. Set aside.

3 Peel the pineapple, remove and discard the fibrous center core, and cut the flesh into 1-inch chunks. Place into a bowl and sprinkle with the lemon juice.

4 Add the mango, papayas, and lychees to the pineapple. Remove the leaves from 2 of the mint sprigs, discard the stalks and finely chop the leaves, then stir half the chopped mint into the salad and the rest into the syrup.

5 Just before serving, peel the bananas, slice into chunks, sprinkle with the lemon juice, and add to the salad. Pour the passion fruit syrup over the fruit and serve decorated with the leaves from the remaining mint sprigs and wedges of lime, with single cream.

"Never give up, have the passion. Don't be afraid."
Barbara Broccoli

Fabulous chocolate celebration cake

7oz dark (70% cocoa) chocolate

6 tablespoons milk

1½ sticks (12 tablespoons) unsalted butter, softened

³/4 cup sugar

4 large eggs, beaten

1 ¹/4 cups self-rising flour

½ teaspoon baking powder

1 cup ground almonds

chocolate shavings and/or chocolate shapes of your choice, to decorate

For the ganache

1 cup heavy cream

7oz dark (70% cocoa) chocolate, chopped

Prepare 25 minutes | **Cook** 30 minutes plus 2 hours chilling | **Serves** 6-8

1 Preheat the oven to 350°F. Grease 2 × 8-inch round, loose-bottomed cake pans and line with parchment paper. Break the chocolate into pieces and place in a heatproof bowl with the milk. Rest the bowl over a pan of gently simmering water and leave until melted, stirring frequently.

2 In another bowl, beat the butter and sugar until pale and creamy. Stir in the eggs, flour, baking powder, and almonds. Add the melted chocolate and stir until evenly combined. Divide between the prepared pans, level the surfaces, and bake in the oven for 25–30 minutes or until just firm. Remove from the pans and cool on a wire rack.

3 For the ganache topping, heat the cream in a small heavy-bottomed pan and heat until steam rises and bubbles appear around the edge, and stir in the chopped chocolate. Leave until melted then transfer to a bowl and chill in the fridge for 1½ – 2 hours, until the mixture is just thick enough to hold its shape.

4 Now assemble the cake. Place one of the cake layers on a plate, then spread with about a third of the chocolate ganache. Top with the second layer. Spread the remaining ganache over the top and sides, swirling with an offset spatula. Decorate with chocolate shavings or chocolate shapes of your choice. Keep in a cool place.

"Women have a great ability to build connections that ultimately make great things happen."
Nicky Kinnaird

Mini chocolate meringues

4 egg whites
¼ teaspoon cream of tartar
1½ cups sugar
2 teaspoons cornstarch
1 teaspoon white wine vinegar
1 tablespoons cocoa, sifted, plus
extra for dusting

To serve
whipped cream
fresh raspberries
chocolate spread

I don't believe in getting involved unless you can make a real difference, and with the perfume IN PEACE I had the opportunity to do just that. A percentage of the profits from the sale of it go to Women for Women International's sponsorship program. The women who buy the perfume at Space NK are strong, confident, educated, often family women who have the ability to be self-sufficient—qualities that are not naturally afforded to women elsewhere in the world. On the one hand they know that their purchase will enable women in some of the most volatile countries to take control back for themselves, but the perfume also brings them joy. I feel rather the same about these meringues. They may seem frivolous, but they are a delicious way of re-connecting with our sisters elsewhere.

Prepare 15 minutes | **Cook** 1 hour, plus 30 minutes cooling | Makes 30-35

1 Preheat the oven to 285°F. Line 2 baking sheets with nonstick parchment paper.
2 Place the egg whites with the cream of tartar in a really clean and grease-free bowl, and whisk with an electric whisk until they hold their shape and form soft peaks. Add half the sugar, spoon by spoon, continuing to whisk until the meringue is glossy and thick. Fold in the remaining sugar with a large metal spoon, followed by the cornstarch and the vinegar. Swirl the cocoa randomly through the meringue.
3 Using a piping bag or teaspoon, spoon or pipe small blobs of the meringue (about 60–70 depending on the size—it needs to be an even number if you're going to sandwich them) onto the parchment paper, keeping them all the same size and shape. Bake in the oven for 50–60 minutes, turn the oven off ,and then leave to cool in the oven with the door slightly open. Let the meringues cool completely before carefully removing them from the paper.
4 Serve a few with soft peaks of whipped cream and fresh raspberries, or sandwich together in pairs with whipped cream or chocolate spread, dusted with cocoa.

> *"We are inspired to help change the structural causes of poverty because there is more than enough to go around if only the rich and the corporations didn't rig the system in their favor."*
>
> **Ben & Jerry**

Baked alaska ice cream

8-inch round white cake layer
4 egg whites
³/₄ cup sugar
1 teaspoon cornstarch

For the ice cream
2 cups (8oz) fresh raspberries
5 tablespoons confectioners sugar
6 large egg yolks
¹/₃ cup sugar
2½ cups milk
1¹/₄ cups heavy cream
2 vanilla pods, split
2 × chocolate honeycomb bars, like Butterfingers or similar, chopped

Prepare 30 minutes, plus up to 11 hours freezing | **Cook** 20 minutes | **Serves** 8

1 First, make the ice cream. Place 1 heaping cup of the raspberries in a fine strainer over a bowl and press them through with the back of a spoon, discarding the seeds. Sweeten with the confectioners sugar, adding more to taste if necessary.

2 Put the egg yolks in a bowl with the sugar and mix to combine. Heat the milk with the cream and vanilla pods until nearly at boiling point, then pour into the eggs, stirring continuously to make a custard. Rinse the milk pan and strain the custard back into the pan, discarding the vanilla pods. Return the pan to medium heat and heat gently, stirring continuously, until thickened and coating the back of a spoon. (This will take a good 10 minutes, so be patient, otherwise you'll end up with scrambled eggs.) Strain the custard back into a clean cold bowl and cover with waxed paper to prevent a skin forming. Leave to cool.

3 Once the custard is cool, churn in an ice cream machine according to the instructions, until thick and smooth. (Or pour into a freezer-proof container and place in the freezer. After 2 hours, whisk the ice cream to break up the crystals, repeating this 3 or 4 times until the ice cream is thick and smooth.) Gently swirl in the raspberry purée, remaining raspberries, and chocolate chunks.

4 Meanwhile, line the inside of a freezer-proof, 6-cup bowl with plastic wrap. Spoon the ice cream into the bowl, packing it in and pressing in down with the back of the spoon to compact it, then level the surface and cover with the disk of cake, trimmed if necessary to fit the bowl. Cover and place in the freezer for at least 1–2 hours, or until the ice cream is solid.

5 Whisk the egg whites in a thoroughly clean bowl until softly peaking. Gradually spoon in the sugar and cornstarch, whisking well after each addition until all the sugar is added and the meringue is stiff and glossy.

6 Loosen the edges of the ice cream with a warm knife and remove from the basin. Invert onto a baking sheet. Using an offset spatula, spread the meringue over the top and sides, completely encasing the ice cream in a generous but even layer. Rough up the surface and place in the freezer for 1 hour or until required.

7 Just before serving, preheat the oven to 450°F. Place the baking sheet in the oven for about 3–4 minutes, until the meringue is turning golden-brown. Watch carefully because the meringue browns and ice cream melts quickly. Transfer from the baking sheet to a serving plate and serve immediately!

contributors

The people listed below, from chefs to celebrities to humanitarians, have all contributed a recipe to this book. They also give their time and support to various charities and causes. We would like to thank them for taking part in this project, and for sharing their recipes with us.

Tindyebwa ("Tindy") Agaba

Recipe © Beef Stroganoff page 156

Muryango

A former child refugee, Tindyebwa has established a social entrepreneurship movement called Muryango that works with young refugees in Egypt and ex-combatants in Liberia, helping them become more productive in their respective societies. He believes that African youth affected by conflict are best served and can lead more fulfilling lives if they are given the opportunity to stay in their local communities.

Stephanie Alexander

Recipe © Mary's rabbit pie page 159

Stephanie Alexander Kitchen Garden Foundation (www.kitchengardenfoundation.org.au)

Stephanie Alexander is the bestselling author of 14 books, including *The Cook's Companion*, regarded as an Australian classic. She was a Melbourne restaurateur for more than 30 years. In 2004, she established the Stephanie Alexander Kitchen Garden Foundation, a not-for-profit organizaton that aims to teach primary school children about food through example and positive experience. The movement has grown to include 267 Australian primary schools, and is supported by the Australian Government, the Victorian State Government, the Queensland State Government, corporate partners and philanthropic support. Stephanie was awarded an Order of Australia in 1994.

Manal Alsharif

Recipe © Basbosa page 120

My Right to Dignity (www.myright2dignity.com)

In 2011, Alsharif defied authorities and posted a video of herself driving on YouTube and Facebook. She has been imprisoned numerous times but continues to campaign for women's rights in Saudi Arabia.

Christiane Amanpour

Recipe © Lemon, garlic and rosemary roast chicken page 89

The Cherie Blair Foundation (www.cherieblairfoundation.org)

The global affairs anchor at ABC News, host of *Amanpour* and chief international correspondent for CNN International, Christiane Amanpour's illustrious career spans three decades. She has reported from all the world's major hotspots, including Afghanistan, Iraq, Iran, Pakistan, Somalia, Israel, the Palestinian territories, Asia, Rwanda and the Balkans, and interviewed most of the top world leaders, including securing the only interview with Hosni Mubarak and an exclusive with Muammar Ghadafi during the Arab Spring. The recipient of every major broadcast award, including an inaugural Television Academy Award, nine News and Documentary Emmys, four George Foster Peabody Awards, and nine honorary degrees, she is also an Honorary Citizen of Sarajevo.

Helen Bamber OBE

Recipe © Piperade page 31

Helen Bamber Foundation (www.helenbamber.org)

Starting in the German concentration camp of Bergen-Belsen after WWII, Helen Bamber has worked tirelessly for human rights for over 60 years. An early member of Amnesty International, she established The Medical Foundation for the Care of Victims of Torture in 1985, where she remained a guiding light until 2005. Named European Woman of Achievement in 1993, she was awarded an OBE in 1997 and in the same year received a lifetime Human Rights Achievement award. She is founding co-director of the Helen Bamber Foundation, which treats survivors of human trafficking, former child soldiers and women who have suffered genital mutilation, whose traumas often remain undiagnosed and untreated.

Maggie Beer

Recipe © Chicken with vino cotto page 217

McCusker Alzheimer's Research Foundation Inc. (www.alzheimers.com.au)

One of Australia's best-known food personalities, Maggie Beer's first restaurant, the Pheasant Farm, was awarded the Remy Martin Cognac/Australian Gourmet Traveller Restaurant of the Year award in 1991. These days, her career spans farming and food production, as well as television presenting and food writing. She is proud to be the South Australian Ambassador for the Stephanie Alexander Kitchen Garden Foundation. Among her many awards are Senior Australian of the Year 2010 and Senior South Australian of the Year 2011. She is also a Member of the Order of Australia (AM) for her service to tourism and hospitality in 2012.

Ben & Jerry

Recipe © Baked alaska ice cream page 235

Ben & Jerry's Foundation (www.benandjerrysfoundation.org)

Childhood friends Ben Cohen and Jerry Greenfield started Ben and Jerry's Ice Cream in 1978 in an old gas station on an investment of $8,000. Ben and Jerry's developed a unique values-led business model, went public, and grew to $300 million before it was acquired by Unilever in 2000. Cohen and Greenfield are the recipients of numerous awards for their commitment to social responsibility, including the US Small Business Award, James Beard Humanitarians of the year, and the Peace Museum's Community Peacemakers of the year awards. Ben and Jerry are also the recipients of several honorary doctorates and the authors of several books. Today, Ben is the Head Stamper of StampStampede.org, a campaign to amend the Constitution to get money out of politics through the joy of rubber stamping paper currency. Jerry is currently the President of the Ben & Jerry's Foundation.

Marco Borsato

Recipe © Individual carrot cakes page 61

War Child (www.warchild.org)

One of the most successful singers in the Netherlands, Marco Borsato has had 14 No. 1 singles, 6 No. 1 albums and 4 No. 1 DVDs, and hundreds of thousands flock to his concerts. Since 1998, he has worked tirelessly as an ambassador for War Child, visiting projects all over the world and mobilizing people to contribute to the charity's mission: a peaceful future for all children. War Child is one of the Netherlands' best-known charities. Borsato's commitment also led to the production of the award-winning movie *The Silent Army*, which focuses on the issue of child soldiery.

Sir Richard Branson

Recipe © Spaghetti bolognese page 77

The Elders (www.theelders.org) Virgin Unite (www.virginunite.com)

Sir Richard Branson founded Virgin as a mail order record retailer in 1971. Today, the Virgin Group consists of approximately 200 companies in over 30 countries. Through Virgin Green Fund, the group is investing in renewable energy and resource efficiency. In 2007, they announced the Virgin Earth Challenge – a $25 million prize to encourage a viable technology which will result in the net removal of anthropogenic, atmospheric greenhouse gases. Also in 2007, Sir Richard joined Peter Gabriel, Nelson Mandela, Graça Machel, and Desmond Tutu to form The Elders, a group of world leaders, to contribute their wisdom, leadership and integrity to tackle some of the world's toughest problems. Virgin Unite, the group's not-for-profit foundation, focuses on entrepreneurial approaches to social and environmental issues.

Dr. Holly Branson

Recipe © Spaghetti bolognese page 77

Free The Children (www.freethechildren.com)

The daughter of Sir Richard and Lady Joan Branson, Dr. Holly Branson joined the Virgin Group in 2008, using her medical experience to help Virgin set up health clinics in Africa and to work alongside Virgin Unite to raise awareness of health issues. In 2010, Holly, along with her brother, Sam, formed Team Caterpillar, which involved enlisting 32 of their friends to complete the first ever Virgin Money London Marathon while raising £284,000 for their various charities.

Sam Branson

Recipe © Spaghetti bolognese page 77

Big Change Charitable Trust
www.bigchangecharitabletrust.org

In 2007, Sam Branson traversed 1,200 miles across the Arctic on a dogsled to raise awareness of climate change. His passion for the environment was cemented by this experience, with the Inuit's struggle against their changing landscape giving continuing inspiration. In 2009, he set up Sundog Pictures, a production company created with the specific ambition to deliver challenging, entertaining and informative films and television programs, through which he hopes to inspire social change.

Emma Bridgewater and Matthew Rice

Recipe © Cheese and leek tart page 196

Emma Bridgewater and her husband, Matthew Rice, design every piece of Emma Bridgewater pottery themselves. Everything is made by hand in a Victorian factory in Stoke-on-Trent, keeping the area's traditional skills alive and ensuring that each piece has a real integrity. Emma and Matthew are passionate about halting the near terminal decline of the ceramics industry, and strive to create a vibrant, dynamic work environment for their employees. The café at the factory provides visitors with locally grown food, along with produce from two greenhouses heated by the kilns in the factory below. Both Emma and Matthew are passionate about the traditional skills and surroundings of Stoke-on-Trent and have recently planted 5 acres of derelict land next to the factory with wild flowers to benefit birds and insects.

Barbara Broccoli

Recipe © Fabulous chocolate celebration cake page 231

Barbara Broccoli, OBE is a film producer and long-term supporter of Women for Women International. Together with her brother, Michael G. Wilson, she has produced every Bond film since Goldeneye. Barbara is the Chair for First Light, UK's leading filmmaking initiative for young people. In 2012, Barbara arranged an auction of Bond memorabilia with Christie's which raised £1,641,350 for charities including Women for Women International and UNICEF.

Jennifer Buffett

Recipe © Kale salad page 202

Women for Women International
(www.womenforwomen.org)

Jennifer Buffett's philanthropic work began in 1997 when her parents-in-law, Susan and Warren Buffett, bequeathed Jennifer and her husband, Peter Buffett, a small charitable fund. Today she leads the NoVo Foundation, which seeks to empower girls and women as primary agents of change, and to end violence against them. Jennifer also serves on the boards of the Nike Foundation, V-Day, CASEL (Collaborative for Academic and Social and Emotional Learning), BRAC USA and Apne Aap Women Worldwide. Jennifer and Peter are recipients of the Clinton Global Citizen Award for their "visionary leadership and sustainable, scalable work in solving pressing global challenges." In 2010, she was selected by ex President Clinton to be a founding member of the Clinton Global Initiative's young global leaders cohort, "CGI LEAD," n 180 nations.

Alex Cooke

Recipe © Pot-roasted silverside with shallots page 86

Love Russia (www.loverussia.org)

Alex and his wife, Jaqui, have run Love Russia since 1999. Love Russia is a small charity established to improve the lives of thousands of orphaned and abandoned children and young people living in Russia. They have been involved in over 600 projects that focus mainly on children but also provide care for the elderly and those that are disabled or have learning difficulties. Their aim is to provide relief of poverty, suffering and distress. Love Russia has gained the reputation of being the "ones that come back"—again, and again, and again. They believe it is this trust that is the secret of working effectively.

Jesse Ziff Cool

Recipes © Slow-cooked pork with potatoes and greens and Cabbage and pepper slaw with ginger page 215

Partners in Health (www.pih.org)

Passionate about healthy food and caring for local farmers, Jesse Ziff Cool opened one of the first organic restaurants in the United States in 1976. Over the years she held true to "creating delicious nourishing food from the best sources" and today owns three successful restaurants, as well as a catering company in California's Silicon Valley. The author of seven cookbooks, she is dedicated to the politics of sustainable agriculture and farm to table cuisine. At her home garden and kitchen, Jesse works with Stanford's Department of Education inspiring elementary student teachers on how to build curriculum from the garden to the table. She is a consultant for Stanford Hospital having created an organic, healthy food menu for hospital patients. Jesse has worked in the local community throughout her career to share the joy of cooking through teaching and by providing job opportunities and skills to less fortunate members of society. In 2012, she expanded her teaching to include Rwandan participants of WfWI's cooking program. In 2013, Jesse will join Eve Ensler's V-Day Uprising "Power to the Women and Girls of the DRC" in support of women and families in Congo at City of Joy.

Ann Cooper

Recipe © Fresh sweetcorn chowder page 69

Food Family Farming Foundation
(www.foodfamilyfarming.org)

Ann Cooper is a celebrated author, chef, educator and enduring advocate for better food for all children. A Director of Food Services for the Boulder Valley School District, she is co-founder of Lunch Lessons LLC and the Food Family Farming Foundation(F3)'s Lunch Box Project: Healthy Tools for All Schools. F3 is also the managing partner of the Let's Move Salad Bars to Schools initiative, working to donate 6,000 salad bars to American schools by 2013. In a nation where children are born with shorter estimated life expectancies than their parents because of diet-related illness, Ann is a relentless voice of reform by focusing on the links between food, family, farming and children's health and wellness.

Peter Davis

Recipe © Braised goat or lamb with greens and corn page 166

Share our Strength
(www.nokidhungry.org)

Honored by The James Beard Foundation as one of "The Best Hotel Chefs in America", Peter Davis has been recognised nationally for his commitment to sustainable agriculture. An avid conservationist with close ties to the fishing and farming communities of New England, and a true working chef, he is heavily involved in the daily operations of his restaurant Henrietta's Table. He was also one of the first proponents of the use of organic products, and will not use any genetically engineered foods or products.

Dame Judi Dench

Recipe © Bread and butter pudding page 115

Cancer Research UK
(www.cancerresearch.uk.org)
Cystic Fibrosis Trust (www.cftrust.org)

Probably best known internationally for her role as "M" in the James Bond films, Dame Judi Dench has received popular and critical acclaim for an outstanding career in both classical and contemporary roles, winning numerous major awards for work on stage and screen, including an Academy Award, nine BAFTA awards and six Laurence Olivier awards. In recognition of her achievements, she received an OBE in 1970, became a DBE in 1988, and in 2005 was awarded a Companion of Honor. She is a patron of around 250 charities, including the British Lung Foundation, Cancer Research, Cystic Fibrosis Trust, British Heart Foundation, Help the Aged, Action for Children, several charities for the blind, as well as many others including theatrical and animal charities.

Fraser Doherty

Recipe © Easy jam-filled cookies page 179

CEO of SuperJam, a company he started when he was 14 years old in 2004 by selling his homemade jams door to door, Fraser Doherty has invested in numerous charitable projects, supports mentoring programs and speaks to Scottish school children encouraging entrepreneurial pursuits. SuperJam Tea Parties, the charity he established in 2008, hosts tea parties for elderly people who live alone or in care homes. The company also organises various "knitathons," encouraging the public to knit for good causes. In 2008, several thousand knitted squares were collected, sewn into blankets and sent to orphanages in India.

Maria Eitel

Recipe © Kleftiko (Greek roast lamb) page 225

The Girl Effect (www.girleffect.org)

Instigator of the 'Girl Effect', Maria Eitel is the founding CEO and President of the Nike Foundation. She leads the Foundation's efforts to put girls on the global agenda and drive resources to them with the goal of eradicating global poverty. The work of the Nike Foundation is supported by Nike, Inc. and the NoVo Foundation, a collaboration that has enabled the impact of the Girl Effect to grow exponentially. She is a regular speaker at local, national and global forums on corporate responsibility, governance, human and labour rights, sustainable development, philanthropy, and social entrepreneurism.

Mia Farrow

Recipe © Breakfast pancakes page 59

The Darfur Archives (www.sudan.uconn.edu/farrow_darfur_archives.htm)

A critically acclaimed actress who has appeared in more than 40 films, as well as on the stage and television, Mia Farrow is equally well known as a tireless advocate for human rights. Her primary focus has been on conflict-affected regions in sub-Saharan Africa. She has travelled to the Darfur region of Sudan more than a dozen times and has written and spoken extensively about the genocide. In 2008, she was selected by *Time* magazine as one of the most influential people in the world. In 2009, she undertook a hunger strike to protest against the expulsion of humanitarian agencies from the Darfur region. She is currently working on her own project, The Darfur Archives, documenting the cultural traditions of Darfur's major ethnic tribes.

Hugh Fearnley-Whittingstall

Recipes © Sticky glazed ribs and Roast squash with chilli, garlic and rosemary page 218

Switchback (www.switchback.org.uk)
ChildHope (www.childhope.org.uk)

A talented writer, broadcaster and campaigner, Hugh Fearnley-Whittingstall is widely known for his commitment to seasonal, ethically produced food and has earned a huge following through his *River Cottage* TV series and books. He and his team are based at River Cottage HQ, a working farm on the Devon-Dorset border, from where they run a broad range of events and courses. His "Fish Fight" campaign to stop the wasteful discarding of dead fish into the North Sea continues to attract a following. He has also worked to raise awareness of commercial chicken rearing versus slow raising of breeds in humane surroundings. Through his "Chicken Out" campaign, he is trying to encourage people to become more aware of food production issues.

America Ferrera

Recipe © Chicken fajitas with sweetcorn salsa page 127

Half the Sky Movement (www.halftheskymovement.org)

America Ferrera is perhaps best known for her portrayal of "Betty Suarez" on the hit comedy *Ugly Betty*, a role that earned her an Emmy, a Golden Globe and a Screen Actors Guild Award. An Artist Ambassador for the global humanitarian organizaton Save the Children, where she focuses on underpriviledged children in the US as well as in third world countries, she has travelled to India with the Half the Sky Movement to visit Urmi Basu and the New Light shelter and is a named patron of the organizaton. She has been honored by the Hispanic Heritage Foundation for being an inspiring role model to Latino youth. Ferrera is also fundraiser and campaigner for Peace First, an organizaton that helps teach youngsters pacifist skills.

Livia Firth

Recipe © Pasta with broccoli, chilli and garlic page 81

Oxfam (www.oxfam.org)
End Child Detention Campaign (www.ecdn.org)

Livia Firth, wife of actor Colin, is a leading advocate for ethical fashion. In 2007, with her brother Nicola Giuggioli, she founded Eco Age Ltd, both a magazine and online shop, and a corporate consultancy boutique, Eco Consultancy. As part of her efforts to promote ethical fashion Livia launched the Green Carpet Challenge in 2010 and started working with leading fashion designers to prove that glamour and ethics can go hand in hand. In 2012 Livia was appointed Oxfam global ambassador, and UN's Leader of Change.

Anne Firth Murray

Recipe © Fruit and nut oaty bars page 53

Global Fund for Women (www.globalfundforwomen.org)

From 1978 to 1987, New Zealander Anne Firth Murray led philanthropic efforts on population and environmental issues for the William and Flora Hewlett Foundation. In 1987, she founded the Global Fund for Women, the largest non-profit organizaton in the world funding women's human rights, and continued to act as president until 1996. In 2005, she was nominated for the Nobel Peace Prize. She is the author of two books: *Paradigm Found: Leading and Managing for Positive Change* and *From Outrage to Courage: Women Taking Action for Health and Justice*.

Matt Flannery

Recipe © Spicy cashew tomato soup page 71

Kiva (www.kiva.org)

Matt began developing Kiva in late 2004 as a side-project while working as a computer programr at TiVo, Inc. In December 2005 he left his job to devote himself to Kiva full-time. The organizaton's mission is to alleviate poverty. Using the internet and a worldwide network of microfinance institutions, Kiva lets individuals lend as little as $25 to help create opportunity around the world. As CEO, Matt has led Kiva's growth from a pilot project to an established online service with partnerships across the globe and hundreds of millions in dollars loaned to low-income entrepreneurs. Matt is a Skoll Awardee and Ashoka Fellow and was selected as one of *FORTUNE* magazine's "Top 40 under 40" list in 2009. In 2011, he was chosen for *The Economist* "No Boundaries" Innovation Award.

Peter Gabriel

Recipe © Cheese soufflé page 195

Witness (www.witness.org) & The Elders (www.theelders.org)

Peter Gabriel began his solo career in 1975, after leaving Genesis, and has since released 11 solo albums, written soundtracks for 3 films and won 5 Grammys. In 1980, he founded WOMAD (World of Music Arts and Dance), which has presented 150 festivals in over 40 countries. In 1989 he conceived and co-founded Witness.org, and was co-founder with Richard Branson of theElders.org, which Nelson Mandela launched in July 2007. He received the Man of Peace award, presented by the Nobel Peace Laureates in 2007, also the "Chevalier dans l'Ordre des Arts et des Lettres" and the "Quadriga" award.

Ruchira Gupta

Recipe © Khatte bharwan karele page 134

Apne Aap (www.apneaap.org)

Ruchira Gupta has worked in India for more than 25 years to end sex trafficking. In 2002, she established Apne Aap, an NGO that since its inauguration has supported over 10,000 women and children trapped in or at risk of prostitution. Countries throughout the world have recognised her work. She is a recipient of the Clinton Global Citizen Award for Commitment to Leadership in Civil Society, and has been honored with the Abolitionist Award by the House of Lords. She received an Emmy Award for Outstanding Investigative Journalism for her documentary, *The Selling of Innocents*.

Ellen Gustafson

Recipe © Apple and berry oaty crumble page 119

The 30 Project (www.30project.org)

A sustainable food system activist, entrepreneur and author, Ellen Gustafson is the co-founder of Food Tank: The Food Think Tank and is currently working on a book with Rodale Press tentatively entitled *We The Eaters*. Food Tank is focused on food system change research and innovation and grew out of Ellen's 30 Project initiative. Ellen also started the ChangeDinner campaign, Co-Founded HealthClass2.0, an in-school health and wellness program, and Co-Founded FEED Projects, a charitable company that has provided over 60 million school meals for children around the world.

Greg Higgins

Recipe © Curried stew of sweet potatoes, pinto beans and cabbage page 163

Chef/owner of Higgins Restaurant & Bar in Portland, Oregon since 1994, Greg Higgins is an avid organic gardener and active proponent of sustainable food practices. He maintains a strong commitment to supporting local farmers, fishermen, ranchers and foragers as well as to educating and inspiring people to choose good, clean food. He was honored by the James Beard Foundation as the recipient of their 2002–2003 Best Chef Award: Northwest/Hawaii.

Julia Immonen

Recipe © Pan-fried fish with a dill, mint & fava bean pilaf page 23

Row for Freedom (www.rowforfreedom.com)

Julia Immonen founded 'Sport for Freedom', which uses the positive power of community and sport to help combat the modern day slave trade. In December 2011, she was part of the first female crew of 5 to row across the Atlantic. Row for Freedom, which sought to increase awareness of the problem of trafficking, was Julia's brainchild and aims to raise £1 million.

Chris Jackson

Recipe © Marathon chicken pesto pasta page 46

Run for Congo (www.justgiving.com/runforcongo)

In 2010, London-based Chris Jackson ran 12 marathons to raise awareness of the crisis and brutality of the conflict in the Democratic Republic of Congo (DRC). Since then, he has continued to be a spokesman on behalf of the women of DRC, and raised vital funds by kayaking the Yukon River. He was named *Cosmopolitan* magazine's Man of the Year in 2011 in recognition of his work.

Ashley Judd

Recipe © Chocolate layer slice page 184

Ashley Judd is an activist and humanitarian at heart. She has travelled the world, spending months in brothels, slums, IDP camps and hospices, doing grassroots, feminist social justice, public health and poverty alleviation work with NGOs on whose boards she serves, such as Population Services International, Apne Aap Worldwide, Demand Abolition and International Center for Research on Women. She is also a Senior Fellow at the Enough Project, which raises awareness about how conflict minerals fuel sexual violence in the Congo. In 2010, she graduated from Harvard's Kennedy School with an MPA. She was awarded the Harvard Law School's Dean's Scholar Award for her paper on Gender Violence: Law and Social Justice.

Najat Kaanache

Recipe © Banana creole cake page 129

Women for Women International (www.womenforwomen.org)

A Spanish-Moroccan chef born in the Pyrenean Mountains of San Sebastian, Najat Kaanache has worked in the world's greatest restaurant kitchens including El Bulli, Noma, The French Laundry, Alinea and Per Se. Her uplifting personal story is one of independence, perseverance, and the determination to be the best against all odds. In Ferran Adrià's words, "Najat Kaanache represents the soul of Morocco through the language of food. Her passion for creativity and innovation are an exemplary reference for the whole country."

Kerry Kennedy

Recipe © Hearty chicken soup page 25

Robert F. Kennedy Center for Justice and Human Rights (www.rfkcenter.org)

An American human rights activist and writer, Kerry Kennedy is the daughter of Robert and Ethel Kennedy. Disturbed by the abuses committed by US government officials against El Salvadorian refugees, she began working in the field of human rights in 1981 and has since led over 40 delegations into places such as El Salvador, Gaza, Haiti, Kenya, Northern Ireland and South Korea. In 1988, she established the Robert F. Kennedy Center for Justice and Human Rights, which seeks to uncover and publicize abuses such as torture, disappearances, repression of free speech and child labor. It also supplies activists with the resources they need to advance their work. She is the chair of the Amnesty International USA Leadership Council, a Director for the US Institute of Peace and Human Rights First, as well as the author of *Speak Truth to Power: Human Rights Defenders Who are Changing Our World*.

Afshan Khan

Recipe © Baghare baingan page 101

Women for Women International (www.womenforwomen.org)
Human Rights Watch (www.hrw.org)
UNICEF (www.unicef.org)

Afshan Khan became CEO of Women for Women International in June 2012, becoming only the second CEO in the organizaton's history. As CEO, Afshan is responsible for setting the strategic vision, mobilizing the necessary financial and other resources to execute that vision, and ensuring that WfWI's work creates the most positive impact possible for women rebuilding their lives after war. Afshan joined WfWI after a career spanning more than 25 years with the United Nations, mainly with UNICEF, most recently as Director of UNICEF's Public-Sector Alliances and Resource Mobilization Office (PARMO). During her tenure in PARMO, she led a team that was responsible for mobilizing more than $10 billion for programs for children and their families from both governments and foundation partners.

Craig Kielburger

Recipe © Kachumbari salad page 147

Free The Children (www.freethechildren.com)
Me to We (www.metowe.com)

A humanitarian, social activist and bestselling author who has inspired a generation of young people to be active change-makers, Craig Kielburger is as the co-founder of Free The Children, the world's largest network of children helping children. The organizaton works with more than a million young people every year, in over 45 countries, and has built more than 650 schools, providing education to over 55,000 children every day. Craig has received the Nelson Mandela Human Rights Award, the World Economic Forum GLT Award, the World's Children's Prize for the Rights of the Child, the Roosevelt Freedom Medal, The Governor General's Medal of Meritorious Service, and the State of the World Forum Award.

Nicky Kinnaird

Recipe © Mini chocolate meringues page 232

In 1993, Nicky Kinnaird opened a shop in the heart of London's Covent Garden. A retail space like no other, it was a browser's paradise designed to showcase a selection of the things she had discovered and coveted. Nicky called it Space NK. Nineteen years later, Space NK is established as one of the most iconic sources of the world's best beauty brands. Its success lies in Nicky's vision of a special space where people gather to share and discover beauty secrets and niche brands with knowledgeable, unbiased and genuinely passionate staff. Space NK is now a corporate sponsorship partner with Women for Women International. Nicky has been instrumental in

contributors

launching the perfume IN PEACE, promoting peace through business, with a percentage of the profits going in to the charity's sponsorship program.

Peter Kindersley

Recipe © Spinach and tomato dahl page 103

An inspirational businessman and pioneer in many fields, Peter Kindersley initially trained as a painter and calligrapher and went on to co-found the internationally successful Dorling Kindersley (DK) publishing empire. In the 1970s, Peter and his wife bought a small farmhouse, high on the Berkshire Downs. They soon began to see the destructive influence of intensive chemical farming on the natural landscape and so they made up their minds to buy the land around them, and make it organic. In 2000 Peter sold DK, and in 2006 took the family's passion for organic living to the world of beauty, with the purchase of Neal's Yard Remedies.

Lauren Bush Lauren

Recipes © Butternut squash soup and Corn bread page 66

FEED (www.feedprojects.com)

Lauren Bush Lauren is the Chief FEEDer and Co-Founder of FEED Projects. Lauren started her work as an Honorary Spokesperson for the World Food Program (WFP) in 2003. Since then, Lauren has taken over a dozen trips to countries around the world with humanitarian agencies to learn about programs that are affectively fighting hunger and malnutrition. In 2005, Lauren designed the initial FEED 1 bag, which feeds one child in school for one year through WFP, as a way for consumers to give back in a tangible and meaningful way. To date FEED has been able to give nearly 60 million school meals to children around the world

Prue Leith

Recipe © Teriyake roast lamb page 221

Stop FGM Now (www.stop-fgm-now.com)

Prue Leith is a restaurateur, caterer, TV cook, broadcaster and food writer. Born in South Africa, she has spent most of her working life in London. After selling her successful food business she focused on humanitarian efforts, helping to found The British Food Trust (which promotes good food), Focus on Food (which teaches schoolchildren to cook), The Hoxton Apprentice (which trains long-term unemployed people to be waiters and chefs) and 3Es Enterprises (which turns around failing state schools). She is currently a trustee of Slow Food UK, which promotes good, fair, clean food under the international Slow Food movement.

Talia Y. Leman

Recipe © Best ever challah page 226

RandomKid (www.randomkid.org)

Talia Leman is the CEO and a Founder of RandomKid, through which she develops ideas, strategies and networks between kids internationally to increase their impact. Having been appointed UNICEF's first known National Youth Ambassador, Talia has worked with kids from 20 countries. She is the winner of numerous international and national awards for her philanthropic work, including the National Jefferson Award for global change along with co-recipients Marlo Thomas and Ruth Bader Ginsberg, and was the subject of a *New York Times* op-ed piece written by Nicholas Kristof entitled "Talia For President."

Gayle Tzemach Lemmon

Recipe © Baba ganoush page 189

ICRW (www.icrw.org)
Dining for Women (www.diningforwomen.org)
We Connect (www.weconnectinternational.org)
Women for Afghan Women (www.womenforafghanwomen.org)

Author of the bestselling *The Dressmaker of Khair Khana*, Gayle Lemmon began as a journalist with ABC news and is now Deputy Director of the Women and Foreign Policy Program at the Council on Foreign Relations. Since 2005, she has been researching women entrepreneurs in conflict and post-conflict regions such as Rwanda, Bosnia and Afghanistan. A contributing editor-at-large at *Newsweek Daily Beast*, she writes regularly on creating jobs in the world's toughest business environments, including Afghanistan and Sierra Leone.

Annie Lennox

Recipe © Porridge page 14

mothers2mothers (www.m2m.org)

Annie Lennox has been named "The Greatest White Soul Singer Alive" by VH1, and one of The 100 Greatest Singers of All Time by *Rolling Stone Magazine*. She earned the distinction of "most successful female British artist in UK music history," selling over 80 million albums, and achieving over 20 international hits across the world, both with the Eurythmics and as a solo artist. In 2003, she was invited to Cape Town, South Africa, to perform for the inaugural concert of Nelson Mandela's 46664 HIV campaign. Moved by the plight of people struggling to cope with HIV in clinics, orphanages, hospitals and townships, she established the SING Campaign to raise funds and awareness, to help prevent the spread of HIV in Africa, most importantly through supporting grass roots organizatons.

Cherie Lunghi

Recipe © Roast pork fillet with five-spice plum sauce page 108

Since graduating from Central School of Speech and Drama, Cherie Lunghi has had a long and fruitful career on stage and in film and television. Well known for her portrayal on television as *The Manageress*, she also appeared in *The Buccaneers, Waking the Dead, Midsomer Murders* and *Secret Diary of a Call Girl*. She has been a member of The Royal Shakespeare Company and The National Theatre. Her film credits include *Excalibur, The Mission* and *Frankenstein*. A long-time supporter of WfWI, she wholeheartedly supports the work they do to empower women to rebuild their lives and their communities, to claim their rights as human beings and plant hope in women's hearts for a better life for themselves and their families.

Nelson Mandela

Recipe © Caranguejo recheado page 209

The Elders (www.theelders.org)

Nelson Mandela has dedicated his life to democracy and equality. He spent 27 years in prison for his role in the anti-apartheid struggle and in 1994 went on to become the first President of post-apartheid South Africa. In 1993, he was named a Nobel Peace Laureate. After stepping down as President in 1999, he continued to work to advance peace, health and human rights in Africa. He has been particularly active in campaigning on HIV/AIDS. In 2007, with the help of Graça Machel and Desmond Tutu, he founded The Elders, a group of 10 independent, progressive leaders committed to building peace and advancing human rights, to work together solving global problems. In 2009, the United Nations adopted Nelson Mandela International Day in celebration of his life and legacy. Fondly known in South Africa by his clan name "Madiba," he remains an inspiration to people around the world fighting injustice and oppression.

David Mayer de Rothschild

Recipe © Sprouts with avocado and lime page 27

A National Geographic Emerging Explorer and a UNEP Climate Hero, David Mayer de Rothschild is an adventurer, environmentalist, author and eternal optimist who founded the Sculpt the Future Foundation, a charity that uses creativity, innovation and storytelling as a way to accelerate social good. From skiing to both the North and South geographical poles, to sailing across the Pacific on a catamaran partially made from reclaimed post-consumer plastic bottles called the Plastiki, David has ventured to some of the most remote and fragile ecosystems in order to bring widespread attention and innovative solutions to urgent global environmental and social issues.

Mary McCartney

Recipe © Hearty pasta and bean soup page 33

**Meat Free Monday
(www.meatfreemondays.com)**

Mary McCartney began her career as a photographer in 1995. Since then, her work has spanned the worlds of portrait and fashion photography. Together with her father, Paul, and sister, Stella, she launched the Meat Free Monday Campaign in 2009 to show everyone the value of eating less meat and how easy it is to do. In 2012, she collaborated with phone maker Vertu and Smile Train, a charity that provides cleft-palate operations for children around the world. Travelling to Beijing and Volgograd, Mary photographed children who have benefited from the rehabilitative surgery provided. The project culminated in a photo exhibition in London, followed by a global tour, raising money and awareness for the organizaton.

Paul McCartney

Recipe © Super vegetable salad page 20

English musician, singer, songwriter and composer Paul McCartney gained world-wide fame with the Beatles. After the group's breakup, he pursued a solo career, later forming the band Wings with his wife, Linda. He has been described as the most successful composer and recording artist of all time by Guinness World Records. He has been a campaigner for animal rights and against genetically engineered foods. He has donated and contributed to numerous charitable projects and performed at some of the most groundbreaking and historic benefit concerts over the years, including Ferry Aid, Band Aid and Live Aid, helping to raise billions for charity. He continues to actively raise money and awareness for The OneVoice Movement, PETA, the Liverpool Institute for Performing Arts, Nordoff Robbins Music Therapy, and the Vegetarian Society.

Allegra McEvedy

Recipe © Barley bits salad with honey'd goat cheese toast page 51

**Fairtrade Foundation
(www.fairtrade.org.uk)**

Allegra McEvedy is a chef, broadcaster, writer and culinary adventurer. Her philosophy is that there are more ways for a chef to make a difference than by winning Michelin stars, and good food should be available to everybody. Described by the *Independent* as "a caterer with a conscience," Allegra was awarded an MBE for services to the hospitality industry, specifically for the promotion of healthy eating and ethical sourcing in the UK. She sits on the advisory board for the Good Catch Sustainable Fish Forum, is a patron of The Food Chain charity, and a patron and ambassador for The Fairtrade Foundation.

Bill McKibben

Recipe © Tandoori yogurt chicken page 97

350.org (www.350.org)

Bill McKibben, a professor at Middlebury College, Vermont, is a writer and activist. Having written the first book for a general audience on global warming, *The End of Nature* (1989), he went on to found 350.org, the first big grassroots group working globally on climate change.

Glynis Murray & Henry Braham

Recipe © Trout with fennel and tarragon page 34

Glynis Murray and Henry Braham, founders of GOOD OIL, first began to grow hemp at their farm in Devon 14 years ago. As well as GOOD OIL, they make GOOD HEMP milk (a healthy alternative to soya milk) and GOOD SEED snacks. Besides growing hemp for food, Henry and Glynis have between them four children, three dogs, three ponies and two donkeys and a couple of day jobs in the film industry (credits include *Nanny McPhee*, *Bright Young Things* and *The Golden Compass*), which is what they do while waiting for the hemp to grow.

Nell Newman

Recipe © Orange scented olive oil almond cake page 54

**Newman's Own Organics
(www.newmansownorganics.com)**

Nell Newman is an environmentalist, biologist and prominent supporter of sustainable agriculture. She and her business partner, Peter Meehan, launched Newman's Own Organics in 1993 as a way to bring organic food into mainstream diets. Originally a division of Newman's Own, the organics division became a separate company in late 2001. The daughter of actors Paul Newman and Joanne Woodward, Nell had an early introduction to natural foods through them at the family's rural Connecticut home. Nell credits her parents with teaching her by example to be socially responsible, politically involved and philanthropic. Newman's Own Organics generates money for Newman's Own Foundation to give away. Since 1982, Paul Newman and the Newman's Own Foundation have donated more than $350 million to educational and charitable organizatons worldwide.

Jamie Oliver

Recipe © Apple berry pie page 183

**The Better Food Foundation
(www.jamieoliver.com/foundation)**

As a phenomenon in the world of food Jamie Oliver is one of the world's best-loved television personalities with programs in over 100 countries. He is also a bestselling author – in 2010, *Jamie's 30-Minute Meals* became the UK's fastest-selling non-fiction book since records began. In an effort to give back to society, Jamie established the Fifteen apprentice program in 2002 to provide professional restaurant training to disadvantaged or unemployed youth. Since then, Jamie has campaigned for better school food and established Jamie's Ministry of Food centers as part of a community-based campaign to teach adults and youth how to cook from scratch. He also set up the Kitchen Garden Project with the aim of teaching children how to grow and cook food. With projects in the UK, USA and Australia, Jamie Oliver has a global family of foundation projects, which aim to inspire, educate and empower people through food.

Yotam Ottolenghi

Recipe © Castelluccio lentils with tomatoes and gorgonzola page 206

**Children of Peace International
(www.childrenofpeace.org)**

Yotam Ottolenghi, chef and co-owner of five bustling restaurants/food shops in London, is one of the most respected chefs in the world. He is the author of the bestsellers *Ottolenghi: The Cookbook* and *Jerusalem*, written with his Palestinian colleague, Sami Tamimi, and *Plenty*. Ottolenghi completed a master's degree in philosophy and literature while working on the news desk of an Israeli daily, but made a radical shift upon coming to London in 1997. He started as an assistant pastry chef at the Capital and then worked at Kensington Place, Launceston Place, Maison Blanc and Baker and Spice, before starting his own group of restaurants in 2002, which were an instant success. Since 2006, Ottolenghi has written a weekly column in the *Guardian*'s weekend Saturday magazine. He presented *Jerusalem on a Plate*, a BBC4 documentary about the food of Jerusalem in 2011 and his 4-part series *Ottolenghi's Mediterranean Feast* aired on More4 in 2012.

Arthur Potts Dawson

Recipe © Roasted eggplant tower with spinach and tomato page 148

Arthur Potts Dawson has created two restaurants described as "sustainably aware urban restaurants," Acorn House and The Water House, and is the chef for the organic "pop-up" restaurant, Mrs. Paisley's Lashings. In 2010, he launched The People's Supermarket, a not-for-profit co-operative social enterprise. The unique business model has its member/owners working voluntarily.

Nora Pouillon

Recipe © Baked fish with three-colored peppers page 160

Nora Pouillon is the chef and owner of Restaurant Nora, which, in 1999, became the first certified organic restaurant in America. A true believer in a sustainable lifestyle, a long-time advocate for organic foods, healthier oceans and environment, and the notion that you are what you eat, drink, and breathe, she has extended this philosophy not only to her restaurant, which celebrates its 34th year in business, but also to her outreach work, which includes serving on the board of directors of seven health and environmental organizatons.

John Prendergast

Recipe © Protein breakfast smoothie page 13

Enough Project (www.enoughproject.org)

A human rights activist and bestselling author, John Prendergast has worked for peace in Africa for over 25 years. The co-founder of the Enough Project, an initiative to end genocide and crimes against humanity affiliated with the Center for American Progress, he has worked for the Clinton White House, the State Department, two members of Congress, the National Intelligence Council, UNICEF, Human Rights Watch, the International Crisis Group, and the US Institute of Peace.

René Redzepi

Recipe © Simple cucumber fermentation page 169

UNICEF (www.unicef.org)

René Redzepi is the chef and co-owner of Noma, a 2-Michelin star restaurant in Copenhagen specializing in Nordic cuisine, named the Best Restaurant in the World by the San Pellegrino Awards in 2010, 2011 and 2012. *Time* magazine also listed Redzepi as one of the 100 most influential people in the world in 2012. A significant number of the restaurant's ingredients are foraged from the parks, woods and shorelines around the city of Copenhagen where the restaurant has developed a network of professional foragers. The staff also forages and all of the people who work in the kitchen go out into the forests and on to the beach as Redzepi believes that if they see how a plant grows and taste it *in situ*, they have a perfect example of how it should taste on the plate.

Mary Robinson

Recipe © Leek and potato soup page 193

Mary Robinson Foundation – Climate Justice (www.mrfcj.org)

The first female President of Ireland (1990–97) and UN High Commissioner for Human Rights (1997–2002), Mary Robinson has been Honorary President of Oxfam International since 2002. A former President of the International Commission of Jurists, she serves on the board of the Mo Ibrahim Foundation and is a member of the Elders, an independent group of global leaders brought together by Nelson Mandela. She also works for the Mary Robinson Foundation – Climate Justice (www.mrfcj.org), an organizaton dedicated to securing global justice for people vulnerable to the impacts of climate change who are usually forgotten – the poor, the disempowered and the marginalized across the world.

Zainab Salbi

Recipes © Beet salad and Celery salad page 201

Women for Women International (www.womenforwomen.org)

Zainab Salbi is the founder of Women for Women International and served as the organizaton's CEO from 1993 to 2011. Her passion for women and their rights to safety and opportunity have meant that close to 400,000 women have, so far, rebuilt their lives in countries affected by conflict. A personal survivor of war, born and raised in Baghdad, Iraq, she has spent the second part of her life in the United States. She founded WfWI with the goal of matching women in need of emotional and financial support with sponsors in another country for one year, and to date has helped to transform the lives of women in Afghanistan, Iraq, Bosnia, Kosovo, South Sudan, Rwanda, Nigeria and the DRC.

In 2011, she was named one of the Top 100 Women Activists and Campaigners by the *Guardian* and feted as a Female Faith Heroine by the Tony Blair Faith Foundation. Also in 2011, *Newsweek* and *The Daily Beast* named her as one of the 100 Extraordinary Women who Shake the World, and she was identified by the Economist Intelligence Unit as one of the most inspirational women in the world. A World Economic Forum Young Global Leader, she was asked by President Clinton to be part of the 22 member CGI lead team and honored by him for her work in Bosnia and Herzegovina in 1993. He also nominated her as one of *Harper's Bazaar*'s 21st Century Heroines to honor her actions, faith and determination in making a difference. She is the recipient of the 2010 David Rockefeller Bridging Leadership Award.

Michelle Sampoerna

Recipe © Indonesian beef rendang page 222

Putera Sampoerna Foundation (www.sampoernafoundation.org)

In 2001, Michelle Sampoerna founded the Putera Sampoerna Foundation, a non-profit organizaton dedicated to improving the quality of and access to education in Indonesia. The Foundation has given thousands of scholarships ranging from primary school up to post graduate university degrees.

Wendy Schmidt

Recipe © Braised broccoli with garlic and lemon page 86

The Natural Resources Defense Council (www.nrdc.org/growinggreen)

As President of The Schmidt Family Foundation, Wendy Schmidt is working to advance the development of clean energy and support the wiser use of natural resources. She is the founder of the 11th Hour Project, Climate Central and ReMain Nantucket, and the co-founder of the Schmidt Ocean Institute. She also serves on the boards of The Natural

Resources Defense Council, The California Academy of Sciences, Grist, The X Prize Foundation and The Cradle to Cradle Products Innovation Institute.

Lisa Shannon

Recipe © Roast vegetables with peanut sauce page 144

A Thousand Sisters (www.athousandsisters.org)

In 2005, after watching an episode of *Oprah* on the plight of women in the Congo, Lisa Shannon founded Run for Congo Women, the first national grassroots movement for Congo. The run series and related media have resulted in more than 11,000 Congolese women's sponsorships through Women for Women International. In 2011, she co-founded Sister Somalia, the first sexual violence crisis center in Mogadishu. Lisa continues her work to build the international women's movement as a full-time, independent writer/activist. She is the author of *A Thousand Sisters*.

Kate Spade

Recipe © Gooey chocolate brownies page 116

New York Center for Children (www.newyorkcenterforchildren.org)

Kate Spade has been working with WfWI since 2005 to promote micro-enterprises for women in the still-recovering communities throughout Bosnia and Herzegovina. Despite Kate selling her business, what began originally as a small program has grown and continued to evolve to a stage where products have been sold in stores to raise money and awareness for WfWI. This innovative partnership has created jobs in Bosnia and Herzegovina, Kosovo, Rwanda and most recently Afghanistan. Kate is now actively supporting the New York Center for Children.

Susan Spicer

Recipe © Sauteed fish with cucumbers, pineapples and chillies page 151

Susan Spicer began her cooking career in New Orleans and opened Bayona, recognised as one of the city's best restaurants, in 1990. She contributes to numerous charity events, such as co-chairing the New Orleans chapter of Share Our Strength's annual "Taste of the Nation" for more than 15 years and has represented New Orleans at the Superbowl hunger-relief fundraiser "Taste of the NFL" since its inaugural year. In May 2010, Susan was inducted into the James Beard Foundation's Who's Who of Food and Beverage in America.

Don and Deyon Stephens

Recipe © Thai green chicken curry page 107

Mercy Ships (www.mercyships.org)

In 1978, Don and Deyon Stephens launched a hugely innovative volunteer-based program providing the world's poorest with free surgery and medical care via a hospital ship.

They now have both fleet and land teams in more than 50 developing countries in Africa, Central America, the Caribbean and the Asia Pacific region, and have expanded training beyond medical services into areas of water and sanitation, agriculture, education and construction. Mercy Ships has donated an estimated £600 million in medical services and over 2.9 million people have been impacted with life-transforming surgeries and ongoing community development..

Meryl Streep

Recipe © Wheatberry salad page 205

Equality Now (www.equalitynow.org)

Within three years of graduating from drama school, Meryl Streep had appeared in a dozen plays in New York, won an Emmy for *The Holocaust* and received her first Oscar nomination. In 2012, in a record that is unsurpassed, she won her 17th Academy Award nomination, and her third Oscar, for *The Iron Lady*. She has pursued her interest in the environment through her work with Mothers and Others, a consumer advocacy group that she co-founded in 1989. M&O worked for ten years to promote sustainable agriculture, establish new pesticide regulations, and increase the availability of organic and sustainably grown local foods. She lends her efforts to Partners in Health, Equality Now and WfWI as well.

Tom Stewart-Feilding

Recipe © Sweet potato-topped salmon and spinach pie page 92

Tom in Tanzania (www.tomintanzania.com)

Since 1999, Tom spends approximately one month each year in Buigiri, a small village in central Tanzania. He is involved in all aspects of helping people improve their living standards – building homes, initiating small income generating projects, distributing meals (tens of thousands to date), facilitating children's education, supplying medicine and items for the disabled. His focus is on the elderly and blind but he helps wherever he can. He pays for all his own costs and receives funding from two schools in England who assist him. Tom is an example of how one person can indeed make a difference.

Trudie Styler

Recipe © Spaghetti al aglio e olio page 45

Rainforest Foundation (www.rainforestfoundationuk.org)

Trudie Styler and her husband Sting founded the Rainforest Foundation in 1989. The Foundation has raised more than $25 million to support indigenous rainforest peoples and help them protect their ancestral lands, and works in more than 20 countries in Africa, Asia, Central America and South America. It has helped local communities protect over 28 million acres of forest – some of the most biodiverse lands on the planet. Trudie Styler is also an Ambassador for Unicef, for which she has raised more than $5.5 million, and an active supporter and contributor to VDay.

Zuhal Sultan

Recipe © Klecha page 180

Musician Zuhal Sultan campaigns to raise awareness of the state of education in Iraq, children's rights and Iraqi culture. At 16, she was named a British Council Global Change-maker and later UNESCO also named her a Young Artist in recognition of her work to promote Intercultural Dialogue between the Arab and Western Worlds. She founded Iraq's first National Youth Orchestra in 2009. The group overcomes geographic, religious and language barriers for 3 weeks annually to learn, practice and perform together internationally.

Aung San Suu Kyi

Recipe © Burmese tomato fish curry page 210

Aung San Suu Kyi, Burma's pro-democracy leader and Nobel Peace Laureate, has come to embody her country's longstanding, peaceful struggle against military rule. In 1988, she returned to Burma after living abroad to find widespread slaughter of protestors against the dictator U Ne Win. As the daughter of prominent Burmese political leader Aung San, she spoke out and initiated a non-violent movement against the military regime. In 1989, the government put her under house arrest where she remained for 15 of the next 21 years. During that time she won the Nobel Prize for Peace (1991). In November 2010, after the election of President Thein Sein, she was released from her third period of detention. In 2012, as chairperson of the National League for Democracy (NLD), Aung San Suu Kyi was elected to Burmese Parliament, where she continues her fight for democracy and freedom for the people of Burma.

Alisa Swidler

Recipe © Quorn and pepper tacos page 75

Sabin Vaccine Institute (www.sabin.org) END7 campaign (www.end7.org)

Alisa Swidler is a leading campaigner across a host of issues in the developing world. In the past 5 years, she has partnered with President Bill Clinton, Sir Richard Branson and Queen Rania of Jordan, and is currently advising Sunny Money, which has the largest sales of solar lights across Africa. Her recent efforts have focused on treating worm-based diseases through mass drug administration throughout India. Alisa is a Trustee of The Walkabout Foundation, Millennium Promise UK, Women Win and The Israeli Fund for UNICEF. She is also on the Advisory Boards of The Lake Tanganyika Floating Health Clinic in Tanzania, One World Futbol, which produces indestructible footballs, and Fonderie 47, a global disarmament initiative. She is the International Brand Ambassador for the ethical couture line, Eden Diodati, and has recently been profiled on www.positive-luxury.com and www.sororitywisdom.com. An American ex-pat, Alisa has lived in the UK for more than 10 years with her husband and five young children.

Emma Thompson

Recipe © Sausage and cabbage bake page 91

Helen Bamber Foundation (www.helenbamber.org)

An Oscar-winning actress and writer, Emma Thompson is chair of the Helen Bamber Foundation. She is co-curator of an interactive art installation—"Journey"—which uses seven transport containers to illustrate the brutal and harrowing experiences of women sold into the sex trade.

Archbishop Desmond Tutu

Recipe © Exotic fruit salad page 228

Desmond Tutu Peace Center (www.tutu.org)

Archbishop Desmond Tutu rose to worldwide fame as an opponent of apartheid in South Africa in the 1980s. The first black South African Archbishop of Cape Town, and primate of the Anglican Church of South Africa, he spoke out against the injustices of the apartheid system and in 1984 he received the Nobel Peace Prize in recognition of his extraordinary contributions to that cause. He is widely regarded as "South Africa's moral conscience." In recent years, he has campaigned against HIV/AIDS, poverty and racism. As a founding member and chair of the Elders, he has been campaigning to end child marriage and support the empower-ment of young girls and women globally. He founded The Desmond Tutu Peace Center, which is committed to creating a society that nurtures tolerance and understanding amongst all people.

Alice Walker

Recipe © Steamed greens with oyster sauce page 108

Alice Walker is one of the most admired African-American writers working today. An accomplished poet, she is best known for her novels, most notably 1982's *The Color Purple*, which won the Pulitzer Prize for Fiction. The book was later made into a successful film. Later novels include *The Temple of My Familiar*, *Possessing the Secret of Joy*, *By the Light of My Father's Smile* and *Now Is the Time to Open Your Heart*. She has also written volumes of short stories and essays, including *You Can't Keep a Good Woman Down* and *In Search of My Mother's Garden*. Walker has taught African American women's studies at Wellesley, the University of Massachusetts at Boston, Yale, Brandeis, and UC Berkeley. She supports antinuclear and environmental causes, and has stood out against the

contributors

oppressive rituals of female circumcision in Africa and the Middle East. Walker has served as a contributing editor of *Ms.* magazine, and she co-founded Wild Trees Press.

Marsha Wallace

Recipe © Oven-roasted tomato, mozzarella and arugula pizza page 139

Dining for Women (www.diningforwomen.org)

Marsha Wallace founded Dining for Women, whose mission is to empower women and girls living in extreme poverty by funding programs that foster good health, education, and economic self sufficiency. The organizaton started with one dinner for 20 women and now has over 8,000 members and has raised over $1.5 million. "Changing the world, one dinner at a time."

Alice Waters

Recipe © Lentil salad with prawns page 42

The Edible Schoolyard (www.edibleschoolyard.org)

Chef, author and the proprietor of Chez Panisse, Alice Waters is an American pioneer of a culinary philosophy that maintains that cooking should be based on the finest and freshest seasonal ingredients that are produced sustainably and locally. In 1996, her commitment to education led to the creation of The Edible Schoolyard. By actively involving a thousand students in all aspects of the food cycle, it is a model public education program that instills the knowledge and values we need to build a humane and sustainable future. Alice Waters is also Vice President of Slow Food International, a non-profit organizaton that promotes and celebrates local artisanal food traditions and has 100,000 members in over 130 countries. She was the Co-recipient, with Kofi Annan, of the Global Environmental Citizen Award, 2008.

Alek Wek

Recipe © Okra stew page 98

UNHCR (www.unhcr.org)

At the age of 14 Alek Wek was forced to flee her homeland of South Sudan to escape the civil war. A model, author and designer, her influence transcends the world of fashion and for over a decade she has lent real support to humanitarian causes. She has spoken at the International Black Caucus Foreign Affairs, serves on the advisory board for the UNHCR, recently spending two weeks in her homeland to help raise awareness of the plight of the refugees, has helped launch the Bracelet of Life campaign in conjunction with Medicins Sans Frontiers, and works closely with AIDS awareness benefits and children's charities through her eponymous charity WEK, which Works to Educate Kids, with the belief that if you educate a kid, you educate a nation.

Judy Wicks

Recipe © Sautéed chicken and mushrooms in a Marsala and sage sauce page 170

Judy Wicks founded the White Dog Café on the first floor of her house in 1983, and grew it into a Philadelphia landmark and a pioneer in the local food movement. Through its non-profit affiliate, Fair Food, White Dog helped other restaurants buy from local farmers. In 2001, Judy co-founded the nationwide Business Alliance for Local Living Economies and founded the Sustainable Business Network of Greater Philadelphia. Judy sold the White Dog in 2009 through a unique agreement that preserves local, independent ownership and maintains sustainable business practices.

Gary White

Recipe © Soda bread page 137

Water.org (www.water.org)

Gary White is CEO of Water.org, which he co-founded with Matt Damon. Water.org is a non-profit organizaton dedicated to empowering people in the developing world to gain access to safe water and sanitation. He is a founding member of the Millennium Water Alliance and WASH Advocates. Gary's entrepreneurial vision has driven innovations in the way water and sanitation projects are delivered and financed, and these innovations now serve as a model in the sector. In March 2009, Water.org received the Skoll Foundation's Award for Social Entrepreneurship and Gary was inducted into the community of Skoll Social Entrepreneurs. In 2009, he was named an advisor to the Clinton Global Initiative. In 2011, *Time* magazine listed him as one of the world's 100 Most Influential People. In 2012, Gary received the World Social Impact Award from the World Policy Institute, and he was also named as one of the Schwab Foundation Social Entrepreneurs of the year.

Greg Wise

Recipe © Thai fish curry page 143

Kyetume Community Healthcare Program (www.kyetumecbhcp.org)

Greg Wise is an actor and carpenter. A number of years ago, he visited the Johnson Nkosi school in rural Uganda—a small primary school catering in the main for AIDS orphans and children affected by AIDS. This school of 250 children mirrored the size of Greg's daughter's school in London, so he set up a twinning between the two, where every child has a pen-pal and can share with each other the joys and hardships of living in both countries. Children from Nkosi have made jewellery, sold at the London school, and the proceeds helped to build a new dormitory and pit latrine. Greg has also been supporting a community-based healthcare organizaton in Uganda, Kyetume Community Based Health Care Program, helping to build a resource center and health center, and most recently a dental facility.

Robin Wright

Recipe © Lettuce wraps page 37

Enough Project - RAISE Hope for Congo (www.raisehopeforcongo.org)

Robin Wright became an internationally recognised actress at the age of 21 after starring as Princess Buttercup in *The Princess Bride*. She is actively involved in the Enough Project's campaign, RAISE Hope for Congo: Protect and Empower Congo's Women. She has spoken in front of Congress and other government officials, educating and imploring action on behalf of the women and girls of Congo. In her speaking and her writing, she aims to create awareness around the international trade in conflict minerals – demanding accountability for the minerals purchased to make electronics products, the sales of which frequently support the deadly militias responsible for much of the violence in the Congo.

Sheryl WuDunn

Recipe © Spinach and fennel risotto page 78

Half the Sky Movement (www.halftheskymovement.org)

Sheryl WuDunn, co-author of *Half the Sky: Turning Oppression into Opportunity for Women Worldwide*, a *New York Times* bestselling book about the challenges facing women around the globe, is the first Asian-American reporter to win a Pulitzer Prize. In 2011, *Newsweek* cited her as one of the "150 Women Who Shake the World." She lectures across the United States and abroad on economic, political and social topics related to women in the developing world, the global economy, China and the emerging market, and also advises entrepreneurs, especially those building a social dimension into their core business.

Muhammad Yunus

Recipe © Piaju page 190

Yunus Center (www.yunuscenter.org)

A Bangladeshi banker, economist and teacher, Muhammad Yunus introduced the world to microcredit and microfinance—loans for individuals too poor to qualify for traditional bank loans, for which he and his bank, Grameen, received the Nobel Peace Prize in 2006, the first Bangladeshi to ever receive this honor. That same year, *Time* magazine listed him as an "Asian Hero" and one of 12 top business leaders worldwide. He has also received many other national and international awards and honors, and, along with Nelson Mandela and Desmond Tutu, was one of the founding members of The Elders. In 2012, *Fortune* magazine cited him as one of the 12 greatest entrepreneurs of the current era, saying his microcredit idea "has inspired countless numbers of young people to devote themselves to social causes all over the world."

Like so many good things, this book began at a kitchen table.

In London, late in 2009, three friends, Lauri, Tracy and Bette Anne, gathered over wine and a warm dinner to share stories. Our conversation led to the experiences we'd shared as "sisters" to women in Rwanda, the Democratic Republic of Congo, Kosovo, Afghanistan and Nigeria—women we were sponsoring through an extraordinary program created by Women for Women International. We had been inspired by the resilience, resourcefulness and, above all, the hope that the women of war had shown us. And despite the extreme contrasts between our experiences, we discovered strong affinity around life's most basic themes: love of family; the desire to be productive and self-sufficient; hope for the next generation; and the understanding that something special, something beyond words, was shared when people gathered in gratitude around a kitchen table. Regardless of ingredients or setting, a home-cooked meal shared a sort of abundance that felt to us—and to our "sisters"—like real nourishment, something much more than just "food." And so this book was born.

We're not saying it was easy. None of we original three had backgrounds in the food industry, let alone publishing. We knew we needed help from creative and culinary experts, which we ultimately found in Ruth and Alison. The many new friends, contributors and colleagues who advised us at every stage helped chart our course. The following three years were filled with endless emails, phone and Skype conversations and—of course—meetings around the kitchen table.

The contributors—whether well-known or not—are all people who, in some way or other, have made a life-long commitment to creating a better world. Some are famed for their cooking—there are recipes from more than 20 international chefs, each of them selected for their commitment to sustainability and organic farming—others are some of the planet's most respected humanitarians, philanthropists, leaders, celebrities and artists. You may recognize many of their names; for those you don't, we encourage you to read their biographies on pages 238–246.

The real jewels, though, are the 14 recipes shared by women from the eight countries in which Women for Women International operates—Bosnia and Herzegovina, Kosovo, the Democratic Republic of Congo, South Sudan, Nigeria, Rwanda, Afghanistan and Iraq. Each of these women was paired for one year with a sponsor through Women for Women International, and has benefited from the support and empowerment of training in business, agriculture, job skills and rights awareness. Rather than living as victims, they have seized the chance to build a better future for their families and communities. They have shared their recipes with joy and a touch of pride—the same spirit with which we share them with you. They've also shared their stories, telling how their lives have been shaped by Women for Women International's one-year training program and sponsorship. By reading their stories and trying their recipes, you are opening your world to others and becoming a participant in a better world, one shaped more by the things we share than by the things that separate us. If this book moves you, as making it has surely moved us, we invite you to consider becoming a sponsor yourself, providing emotional and financial support to a woman in one of the world's war-torn countries for one year. We promise this sponsorship will change her life and possibly your own. We tell how to do that on page 251.

With gratitude

The share team

Lauri Pastrone, Tracy Craighead, Bette Anne Berg, Ruth Tyson and Alison Oakervee

WOMEN for WOMEN
International

"I forget sometimes that I can actually make a difference in the world of another woman so far away."

Patti, sponsor of Esther, Rwanda

What you can do

We hope this book will inspire you to help women survivors of war. Like the *Share* team, you can sponsor a woman to participate in Women for Women International's year-long program of job skills training, rights education and small business assistance, so that she can rebuild her life.

Create a connection with a woman survivor of war

When you become a sponsor, you and your sponsored "sister" embark on a life-changing journey. Your sponsorship gives her access to a year-long, holistic program of life skills classes and vocational training, as well as numeracy and literacy support. In addition, your support will help to cover a stipend she can use to provide her family with basic necessities such as food, medicine, and school fees. When she graduates, the desired outcomes for your sister are that she can sustain an income, that she is well, that she is a decision-maker, and that she has social networks and safety nets.

But more than that, sponsorship is a one-to-one connection. As a sponsor, you can connect with your sister in a very personal way by sending messages directly to her. After experiencing hardship and isolation, receiving a message of support from someone she has never met will inspire your sister to hope for a better future, and to know she is not alone.

"To my sponsor, Patti: I want you to know that I have learnt to make jewellery. I have studied hard and I am already earning an income, thanks to your sponsorship. Even though we have never met, you have been a very good sponsor to me." **Esther**

And while sponsorship is a financial and emotional lifeline for Women for Women International's participants, don't forget how it can impact your life, too. **Liz**, who sponsored Violette from Rwanda, told us, *"I became a sponsor because I wanted to give to others, and I got so much more in return. I just never would have imagined that."*

To sponsor a woman today, please go to https://give.womenforwomen.org/sponsorship

Thank you

For more information, visit www.womenforwomen.org
email sponsorship@womenforwomen.org
or call toll-free 1-888-504-3247 or 202-521-0016

Acknowledgments

We thank Zainab Salbi, Founder of Women for Women International and Lisa Shannon, Founder of Run for Congo Women, the women whose work inspired this book.

A huge thank you to Rupert Thomas, Waitrose Director, marketing and brand development; Ollie Rice, Waitrose editor in chief and Sharon Davis, Waitrose graphic design manager (publications); also to Waitrose Ltd for generously supplying all the food for the photography, for their food expertise and the use of their food editor, Alison Oakervee.

Sincere thanks to Philip Webb, our fabulous food photographer. To food stylists Joss Herd, Danny Maguire and Bianca Nice; stylist Iris Bromet; textile specialist Sally Hutson; photographer's assistant Simon Reed; and recipe tester, Julia Feist. We'd also like to express our gratitude to the Prop House teams at Backgrounds, China & Co, and The Laquer Chest for generously allowing us to use their beautiful props.

Thanks to Gary Anslow, Julie Smith and Paul McBride at Itarus Ltd for their repro magic; and to Mel Walker for all his care and attention to detail. A big thank you to Katie Giovanni for her early faith in the book and the instrumental introductions she made.

Many thanks are also due to Simon Wheeler, photographer and friend, who took beautiful images in Kosovo and Rwanda for the book and encouraged us along the way. To Pam Powers, Elena Bowes and Nicole Weaver for their research and recording of the women's stories. Warmest thanks to chef Jesse Ziff Cool, for her multi faceted and steadfast support of the book.

The following photographers deserve a special mention for the work they have done on behalf of vulnerable people in areas of conflict, and in support of WfWI: Ceerwan Aziz, Robin Cross (Article 25), David James, Heathcliff O'Malley, Lekha Singh, Brian Sokol, Les Stone, and Jenn Warren – your images are beautiful.

Other important contributions were made by: Kathy Belden, Georgia Byng, Cristina Cahill, Siobahn Carolan, Clifford Chance, Tina Constable, Claire Dacam, Lisa Dowdeswell, Wendy Fogarty, Getty Images, Nick Haddow, Becky Hardie, Alexi Hargreaves, Warwick Hewson, Kim Hovey, Mary Clare Jarram, Deborah Johnson, Heather Jones, Ellie Klein, William Klein, Andrew Lamb, Ellen Leanse, David Lidgate, Barbara Linder, Josie McKeith, Tony Morris, Nicola Nolan, O'Melveney & Meyers, Laura Perehinec, Emily Phan Ngo, Phan Tu, Lyndsey Posner, Alice Sherwood, Simmons & Simmons, Alisa Swidler, Samantha Whittaker, Lindy Wiffen of Ceramica Blue and Assumpta Micho (WfWI Rwanda) and all the field staff who responded to our many requests of the local WfWI offices.

Thank you, UK staff of Women for Women International – Nora Russell, Izzy Clark, Sonia Nootan, Mylene Hours, Joeyta Bose, Ilka Noggler, Hollie Montgomery and our committed interns Roisin DeCourcy Wheeler, Sara Priest, Sussan Khatir, and Becca Stahl. And also the UK and US Boards of Directors for WfWI, especially Deborah David, Lucy Billingsley, Christine Fisher, Lady Hannah Lowy Mitchell and Lady Anne Greenstock and board advisor Alfonso Montiel. We are also grateful for the support of Afshan Khan, CEO of Women for Women International.

Our special thank you goes to Brita Fernandez Schmidt, Executive Director of Women for Women International UK. Brita's enduring encouragement and unwavering support were essential to the making of this book.

To Kyle Cathie, we are grateful to you for believing in and investing in this cookbook enough to make it one of your own. Many thanks to Judith Hannam, our brilliant editor, and her assistant, Tara O'Sullivan, for many late nights and great attention to detail.

And finally, our deepest gratitude is saved for our families who have listened, inspired, and supported this book from the very beginning. We love you and thank you!

Lauri, Tracy, Bette Anne, Ruth and Alison x